D1634511

ESSENTIALS
of Managing Treasury

ONE WEEK LOAN

- 3 APR 2009

1 7 FEB 2011

SHEFFIELD HALLAM UNIVERSITY
LEARNING CENTRE
WITHDRAWN FROM STOCK

Essentials Series

The Essentials Series was created for busy business advisory and corporate professionals. The books in this series were designed so that these busy professionals can quickly acquire knowledge and skills in core business areas.

Each book provides need-to-have fundamentals for those professionals who must:

- Get up to speed quickly, because they have been promoted to a new position or have broadened their responsibility scope
- Manage a new functional area
- Brush up on new developments in their area of responsibility
- Add more value to their company or clients

Other books in this series include:

For more information on any of the above titles, please visit *www.wiley.com*

ESSENTIALS
of Managing Treasury

Karen A. Horcher

WILEY

John Wiley & Sons, Inc.

Portions of this work have been used from *Essentials of Financial Risk Management*, Karen A. Horcher; Copyright © 2005, Karen A. Horcher. Reprinted with permission of John Wiley & Sons, Inc.

This book is printed on acid-free paper. ∞

Copyright © 2006 by Karen A. Horcher. All rights reserved.

Published by John Wiley & Sons, Inc., Hoboken, New Jersey.

Published simultaneously in Canada.

No part of this publication may be reproduced, stored in a retrieval system, or transmitted in any form or by any means, electronic, mechanical, photocopying, recording, scanning, or otherwise, except as permitted under Section 107 or 108 of the 1976 United States Copyright Act, without either the prior written permission of the publisher, or authorization through payment of the appropriate per-copy fee to the Copyright Clearance Center, Inc., 222 Rosewood Drive, Danvers, MA 01923, 978-750-8400, fax 978-646-8600, or on the web at *www.copyright.com*. Requests to the publisher for permission should be addressed to the Permissions Department, John Wiley & Sons, Inc., 111 River Street, Hoboken, NJ 07030, 201-748-6011, fax 201-748-6008, or online at *http://www.wiley.com/go/permissions*.

Limit of Liability/Disclaimer of Warranty: While the publisher and author have used their best efforts in preparing this book, they make no representations or warranties with respect to the accuracy or completeness of the contents of this book and specifically disclaim any implied warranties of merchantability or fitness for a particular purpose. No warranty may be created or extended by sales representatives or written sales materials. The advice and strategies contained herein may not be suitable for your situation. You should consult with a professional where appropriate. Neither the publisher nor author shall be liable for any loss of profit or any other commercial damages, including but not limited to special, incidental, consequential, or other damages.

For general information on our other products and services, or technical support, please contact our Customer Care Department within the United States at 800-762-2974, outside the United States at 317-572-3993 or fax 317-572-4002.

Wiley also publishes its books in a variety of electronic formats. Some content that appears in print may not be available in electronic books.

For more information about Wiley products, visit our Web site at *http://www.wiley.com*.

Library of Congress Cataloging-in-Publication Data
Horcher, Karen A.
   Essentials of managing treasury / Karen A. Horcher.
      p. cm.
   Includes index.
   ISBN-13: 978-0-471-70704-2 (pbk.)
   ISBN-10: 0-471-70704-X (pbk.)
   1. Cash management. 2. Finance. I. Title.
   HG4028.C45H67 2006
   658.15'244--dc22

                                        2005019110

Printed in the United States of America

10 9 8 7 6 5 4 3 2 1

For my dear friend Ashley—
you are greatly missed.

Contents

Preface

The subject of treasury management is both broad and deep. Treasury is being revolutionized due to new services and technologies, some of which were only ideas a short time ago. However, technology does not change the nature of treasury. It is still a role that requires proactive risk management and due diligence in the collection and stewardship of organizational assets.

Although there are excellent information sources available on the subject of treasury, this book is designed to be a treasury primer. As a result, it focuses on the major issues and considerations within the evolving world of treasury.

Acknowledgments

There are many individuals who have provided me with opportunity and knowledge. The Treasury Management Association of Canada, through Blair McRobie and his team, as well as his predecessor John Bumister, have been great supporters and have worked hard to further the treasury management profession.

I am very grateful to a number of treasury friends who provided me with guidance and perspective on various matters. In particular, Brian McArthur, Kathy Klopfer, Melanie Rupp, Nick Shepherd, and Peter Weddigen took time out of their busy schedules to provide me with feedback and ideas. Steve ("back to Africa") Farago was quick to respond from an exotic locale. In addition, Stephanie Sharp and Bernice Miedzinski have, over the years, generously provided me with opinions and advice on so many topics. Finally, I am most appreciative that my clients permit me to become involved, in a small way, with their fascinating businesses.

My sincere thanks to Sheck Cho and his team at Wiley for both support and opportunity. And special thanks are reserved for Paul, for his steadfast support through the more demanding parts.

ESSENTIALS

of Managing Treasury

CHAPTER 1

Introduction

After reading this chapter, you should be able to:

- Appreciate the historical impact of past events that have shaped the form and function of today's treasury.
- Understand the component activities of treasury.
- Review the various functions of treasury and how they interact with other parts of an organization.

Background

Over the past several decades, the financial market environment has changed dramatically. Financial market volumes are larger, and news travels more quickly than at any time in history. Governments have always come and gone, crises have erupted, but today the information and implications are almost instant. Events that occur anywhere in the world can impact an organization within minutes.

1

As a result, significant energy and resources today are spent managing the financial implications of internally generated strategies and external events. The historical importance of past events has shaped many of today's treasury activities.

Changes in Financial Markets

Financial markets have changed over the past few decades. A number of factors have contributed, including long-term changes in inflation and interest rates, government debt and deficits, and the increasingly global markets where volatility in one market impacts others immediately.

Following World War I, volatility was a feature of financial markets. By the early 1930s, the financial markets faced some terrible problems, including suspension of the gold standard, massive unemployment, bank failures, and an unprecedented evaporation of wealth. World War II effectively ended the financial outlook of the 1930s as previously idle resources were deployed into war production.

The Bretton Woods Agreement of 1944 concluded the United Nations Monetary and Financial Conference held in Bretton Woods, New Hampshire. The multilateral agreement was designed to foster postwar economic recovery and currency market stability among the nations of the world. Its accomplishments included the beginning of the International Monetary Fund and the International Bank for Reconstruction and Development (the World Bank).

The agreement included pegged exchange rates for the major currencies against the U.S. dollar and a gold price of $35 per ounce, to which the U.S. dollar itself was pegged. As a result, central banks could hold U.S. dollars and be guaranteed the convertibility of their dollars to gold.

The Bretton Woods Agreement would determine exchange rates for the next quarter century, bringing with it foreign exchange market stability.

Today, floating foreign exchange and interest rates provide additional challenges for business at home and abroad. Foreign exchange transactions provide the linkages for international flows of trade and capital. However, with estimated foreign exchange volumes at nearly $2 trillion daily, financial markets can adversely impact organizations transacting business. The impact of global capital flows can be significant, exceeding trade flows and in some cases the economic activity of small countries.

What Is Treasury?

The treasury department is the financial center of an organization. The key role of treasury is the safeguarding and stewardship of an organization's financial assets and the management of an organization's financial liabilities. Treasury's role is often focused on external issues: financial markets, investors, creditors, financial institutions, rating agencies, and debt issuers, for example.

Treasury is responsible for implementing various financial decisions made by management and the board. Its focus is on the financial assets and liabilities of an organization. Treasury also has an important role in risk reduction and mitigation.

In large organizations, a team of professionals might be responsible for various treasury activities. Although many of the functions are more complex within a large organization, smaller organizations may have similar functions domiciled within finance or accounting roles. In a smaller organization, the treasury function may be handled by one or two individuals. Treasury is an integral part of an organization, functioning as a service area to other parts of the organization. Although strategic decisions may be made at the executive level, treasury often plays a key role in advising on alternatives, assessing risk elements, and execution of decisions. The quality of an organization's treasury, therefore, impacts the success of the entire organization.

History of Treasury

The concept of treasury as a store of wealth of a company, a society, or a country is not new. Walter Bagehot, in his 1873 book *Lombard Street: A Description of the Money Market*, wrote about financial institutions and the "ultimate treasury, where the last shilling of the country is deposited and kept."[1]

The role of treasury has evolved significantly over the past 50 years, from a focus on cash management to a more strategic financial focus. Treasury is responsible for bringing a particularly expansive view of finance to an organization, which it gains through its contact with the various parts of an organization, with other financial market participants, and with financial institutions.

The introduction of technology, in particular, has changed the nature of treasury. The ability to electronically extract bank and transaction information, track real-time financial rates and prices, and automate many routine reporting requirements means individuals have an opportunity to add more strategic value. Yet the core of treasury remains the safeguarding and provision of financial assets to the rest of the organization.

The introduction of the Internet to treasury more than a decade ago was nothing short of revolutionary. Even small market participants now have the opportunity for pricing, news, and analytics that had previously been available only to larger participants. Communications

Sheffield Hallam University
Adsetts Library (3)

Borrowed Items 05/10/2015 20:56
XXXX2421

Item Title	Due Date
* Essentials of managing treasury	12/10/2015
Modern financial markets and institutions : a practical perspective	06/10/2015
Corporate finance : principles and practice	11/10/2015
Introduction to accounting and finance	09/10/2015

* Indicates items borrowed today

Library enquiries
Tel: 0114 225 3333 option 3
Items normally renewed automatically
unless requested by another borrower

IN THE REAL WORLD

Notable Quote

Treasury is closely aligned with financial markets through the transactions that an organization undertakes. This quote from more than 100 years ago illustrates that the attributes of a good market have been around a long time:

"A perfect market is a district, small or large, in which there are many buyers and many sellers, all so keenly on the alert and so well acquainted in one another's affairs that the price of a commodity is always practically the same for the whole of the district."

Source: Alfred Marshal, quoted in *The Foreign Exchange Market in the United States*, Federal Reserve Bank of New York, 1998.

networks mean that information can be shared easily between disparate organizations around the world. Treasury technology is discussed in more detail in Chapter 7.

Not so long ago, the business of treasury was synonymous with the activities around cash management, primarily collecting and disbursing cash. Today's treasury is often involved with liquidity management, foreign exchange, and risk management. However, cash and its management remains a central role for treasury.

The changing role of treasury can be seen by its increasing importance as a strategic financial center. Increasingly, treasury functions as a consulting and advisory group to other parts of the organization for activities related to treasury and cash management. Its importance as a liaison with accounting, reporting, and compliance add to its strategic role. In addition, there is more emphasis today on the importance of accurate cash forecasts and management of working capital resources.

Role of Key Participants

The role of treasury is primarily a financial management role. The treasurer's responsibility encompasses cash management, funding, risk management, and relationships with key market participants. In most organizations, the treasurer reports to the chief financial officer (CFO).

A related role is that of controller, who typically also reports to the CFO. However, unlike the treasurer, the controller's role is more focused on accounting and reporting, budgeting, credit, and the audit process. Together, the roles of treasurer and controller provide critical financial support to the business of the organization.

The role of the treasurer and the treasury team has evolved considerably in recent years. Traditionally, the most visible role of treasury was cash management. However, recent events and regulatory changes have focused significantly more responsibility on the CFO, putting more pressure on treasurers.

At the same time, the use of technology to support financial data and reporting has increased dramatically. Reports often are received in near real-time, even from geographically disparate locations. The globalization of commerce has also accelerated dramatically, making it more difficult to view events or situations in isolation. As a result, the treasurer is increasingly seen as a key member of the strategic management team, the global hub focusing on the interrelationship between financial markets and the operations of an organization.

Why Manage Treasury?

Organizations today have much more financial accountability than perhaps ever before in history. Strategy has shifted to support improvements in competitiveness. Without adequate financial management, companies compete in increasingly aggressive global environments without the necessary proficiencies.

Changes have occurred for several reasons. First, management of corporations has become increasingly transparent, and shareholders and stakeholders are aggressive in their demands for adequate financial accountability. Consider, for example, the implications of companies complying with legislation such as Sarbanes-Oxley in the United States.

Second, companies are much more global in their activities. Competitors may be international with a different set of economic circumstances at their disposal. Although organizations can control risk factors internal to the organization, it is not possible to control the many external factors that affect international business activities.

Third, financial markets are arguably more volatile than they were 30 years ago. Changes in exchange rates, interest rates, and commodity prices can quickly and adversely impact a profitable company.

As a result, it is more important than ever to manage treasury and the inherent risks and opportunities appropriately.

Functions of Treasury

Treasury deals with many of the financial risks of an organization. After all, treasury is where major decisions (and mistakes) can be made. In addition, treasury advises on and executes the various strategic decisions of the organization. This responsibility includes obtaining and managing financing and the effective control of funds once financing is obtained, as well as the timely execution of financial decisions made by senior management and the board on behalf of stakeholders.

Treasury encompasses the major functions of cash and liquidity management and financial risk management. Within these two broad categories are several functions.

Traditional treasury functions include cash management, cash forecasting, hedging of financial market exposures, investing, and debt issuance. The management of relationships with financial institutions, such as banks and investment dealers, assessment of acquisitions and divestitures, and other related types of transactions may also be handled by treasury. Treasury may also play an important role in liaison with both the board of directors and senior management.

Organization

The financial function falls into the area of responsibility managed by the CFO. Reporting roles may include vice president of finance, sometimes with a subordinate director or manager of treasury. In large organizations, treasury functions may be handled by several individuals, each with an area of expertise.

Treasury functions vary by industry and organization but typically include cash management, cash forecasting, investing and financing, foreign exchange, information management, reporting, financial institution relationship management, and risk management. In a large organization, these functions may be handled by different groups within treasury. In a smaller organization, individuals may manage treasury with other functions.

Treasury functions on information, and data and system requirements are critical from a strategic perspective. The technology infrastructure permits an organization to have adequate information and reporting to make key financial decisions.

Cash Management

Cash management plays an important role in an organization, and it is the central role for treasury. Most other treasury functions develop as a result of cash management. Cash management includes cash flow forecasting, control of cash receipts, and disbursements. The investment of excess cash and funding or debt issuance to cover cash shortages are also considered to be under the broad label of cash management, as are the analysis and control of cash balances.

Cash flow forecasting, in particular, is an important aspect of treasury. There are many benefits to an accurate cash flow forecast, both short term and long term. Many senior executives consider an accurate cash flow forecast and the availability of adequate liquidity to be the most valuable contributions that treasury makes to an organization.

Risk Management

Financial risk management is the process of dealing with the uncertainties that arise from financial markets. Although the process of financial risk management incorporates aspects that are unique to specific industries and organizations, there are some universal components. These include:

- Identification of key risks, including risks that arise from financial markets, extension of credit, and the ability to obtain financing

- Procedures for risk measurement

- Development of alternative risk management strategies

- Determination of risk appetite or tolerance

- Formation of, and contribution to, financial risk management policy

- Implementation of risk management strategies
- Development of infrastructure to monitor risks and report on compliance with policies and performance reporting

Treasury provides a valuable role in the process of risk management, advising senior management and the board on whether to hedge, what to hedge, how to hedge, and the implications of hedging decisions. The most common risk management activities in treasury include foreign exchange, interest rates, credit, operational issues, and commodity prices. Treasury risks are discussed in more detail in Chapter 6.

Other Treasury Roles

Other treasury roles include bank and counterparty management, and technology, services, and infrastructure support. Treasury also acts as a strategic advisor to management, providing information about financing opportunities, cash flow forecasts, and financial asset valuation.

Because many treasury professionals have financial market expertise, it is not surprising that treasury often provides market intelligence, both locally and globally. Analysis and performance benchmarking and reporting are other areas in which treasury contributes to the long-term benefit of an organization.

Treasury Community

An organization's treasury depends on a number of key and ancillary community members, including:

- Financial institutions, including banks and dealers
- Investment community

- Regulatory environment that dictates reporting and accounting requirements

- Accounting, audit, and legal experts

- Vendors of information or infrastructure, including payments, data, and software

- Credit rating agencies

Externally, treasury relies on organizations such as accounting and legal professionals, as well as financial institutions. Many of treasury's most important relationships are with financial institutions.

The management of key relationships is a role that naturally falls to treasury due to its extensive contact with many of these organizations. Treasury manages the relationships with financial institutions and the investment community, as well as the rating agencies that facilitate the reports that ease the debt issuance process.

Financial Institutions

Financial institutions function as financial intermediaries, delivering various financial services and facilitating nonfinancial activities. Financial institutions may act as principals, buying or selling currencies, debt, or investments for or from their own account. They may also act as brokers, in which case a commission for buying or selling may be payable. Services provided by financial institutions include:

- Processing receipts and disbursements

- Debt issuance

- Investments

- Foreign exchange products and services

- Hedging products, including derivatives

- Custodial and trustee services

Financial institutions provide varied services through in-house experts, whose skills and relationships are managed by the account manager or relationship manager assigned to an organization. The need for a new type of service—to discuss interest rate swaps, for example—should be prefaced by a call to the relationship manager, who can direct treasury to the appropriate person and follow up to ensure all documentation is in place to transact business.

Although financial institutions often provide informal advice to treasury, their main area of expertise is their own portfolio of products and services. As a result, their understanding of each organization and its unique attributes may be limited. Financial institutions are discussed in more detail in Chapter 8.

Investment Community

The external investment community is an important one for many treasuries, particularly if the organization issues marketable debt to investors, either through an investment dealer or directly to the marketplace. The investment community includes rating agencies, which are important components of the investment mechanism.

Credit rating agencies provide credit assessments of borrowers, financial institutions, governments, and debt issuers. Prominent credit rating agencies include Dominion Bond Rating Service, Fitch, Moody's Investors Service, A. M. Best, and Standard & Poor's Ratings Services.[2] Credit risk is discussed in more detail in Chapter 6.

Service Providers

Other participants that provide key or important products and services to treasury include consultants, who may work on specific projects or provide ongoing advisory services, real-time information providers, payment facilitators, and vendors and developers of treasury and related software. These are discussed in more detail in Chapters 7 and 8.

Treasury and the Organization

Treasury operates a financial clearinghouse for all other parts of an organization. In large companies, an international or regional treasury may provide specific services to companies within the corporate group anywhere in the world.

Just as all parts of an organization typically impact treasury, either directly or indirectly, the efficient and effective functioning of treasury provides implicit benefits throughout an organization. As a result, the organization may benefit from lower cost of funds, debt reduction, control of risk, increased liquidity, and the benefit of strategic financial planning expertise.

Sales transactions with customers and clients affect treasury through the collection of funds, normally accounts receivable. Purchases of raw materials, services, and goods for resale also affect treasury through payments and accounts payable.

Other departments that affect treasury include human resources, through salaries and wages, benefits, and bonuses. The legal department may provide information about claims that have been made or are being settled or significant financial settlements, such as the purchase or sale of real estate. The tax department will have to submit regular payments for taxes. The executive office may have information about potential acquisitions, divestitures, or mergers. These activities can have a significant impact on treasury.

Summary

- Treasury is an important component of the success of an organization. A well-run, efficient treasury provides benefit to many parts of an organization, freeing other divisions to focus on creating and delivering a better product and to capitalize on opportunities as they arise.

- The business of treasury includes a number of functions, the most important of which are cash management and risk mitigation. Within those broad categories are cash forecasting, investing, debt issuance, foreign exchange, hedging, and managing bank relationships.

- Treasury depends on other professionals and organizations for its smooth functioning. A good understanding of the business of treasury and its unique challenges by professionals throughout an organization helps it to function effectively.

Notes

1. Walter Bagehot, *Lombard Street: A Description of the Money Market* (London: H. S. King & Co., 1873).
2. These rating agencies are recognized by the Securities and Exchange Commission as nationally recognized statistical rating organizations (NRSRO) as of June 2005.

CHAPTER 2

Cash Management

After reading this chapter, you should be able to:

- Understand the key issues with respect to collection and disbursement of cash.
- Identify methods to reduce underutilized cash assets.
- Evaluate global cash management issues and considerations.

What Is Cash Management?

Cash management is the forecasting, control, and stewardship of an organization's financial assets, protecting them from fraud, error, or loss. Cash management is a critical component of liquidity management, without which most organizations have serious difficulty operating.

Treasury plays an important role in the cash management function, including:

- Accurately forecasting timing and amount of cash flows
- Controlling disbursements and speeding collections of cash
- Protecting cash from fraud, error, or loss
- Arranging funding to cover temporary and longer-term cash shortfalls
- Investing excess cash with a focus on minimizing risk, maximizing return, and ensuring liquidity

These functions are discussed in this and subsequent chapters.

Cash Forecasting

Cash forecasting is a key service provided by treasury. In fact, many chief executive officers (CEOs) consider the management of liquidity and the accuracy of cash forecasts to be the most valuable contribution treasury makes to an organization. Therefore, the importance of cash forecasting should not be underestimated.

Cash management starts with an accurate forecast of present and future cash flows. Forecasting accuracy is important because numerous financial decisions are based on the forecast. One of the critical treasury roles is the management of current and future cash balances.

The format and level of detail required in a cash forecast depends to a great degree on the user of the forecast. A senior manager or project leader may require only summary data by week, by month, or by quarter. A money market trader who is investing the corporate cash portfolio may require more detail and granularity, with a likely time interval of daily. Cash forecasts that are used to reconcile actual against forecast transactions will require the greatest level of detail.

In most cash forecasts, cash inflows are segregated from cash outflows. The number of categories of each will vary depending on the organization's own requirements. Some forecasters prefer a minimum of categories, choosing to delve further into the numbers if they require more detail. Other forecasters prefer more detail at a glance. It is sometimes suggested that the vertical size of the forecast should fit for viewing on a normal computer monitor to avoid scrolling up and down and for legibility on a printed page.

The technology used to build a cash forecast may also dictate the way that it is structured. The use of a database, as compared with a spreadsheet, provides additional flexibility. The forecast built using a cash flow database permits reformatting data for different users.

Forecasting Methods

There are several methods for determining the cash flows that make up a cash forecast. Depending on the organization and the individuals involved in forecasting, a formal approach to forecasting may be appropriate, using historical data and statistical analysis. In other organizations, cash flow forecasting may be based on the experience and knowledge of the cash forecaster. In many cases, experience and internal organizational knowledge may result in forecasts that are accurate. However, this approach does not provide a backup if the employee retires or is transferred to another part of the organization.

Scheduling   The simplest, and usually the first, approach to forecasting is scheduling large-value or discrete cash inflows or outflows.

These are cash flows that either will occur or will not occur, but they typically do not partially occur. For example, a wire payment is forecast to occur on a particular day. If for some reason the payment is not initiated, it will not be paid. Scheduling is used for cash flows that are of material amount for the organization.

Distribution   The distribution method is often used for check clearings or trade receivables, where an amount is likely to occur but the amount is not known with certainty. Distribution is used for forecasted amounts that consist of a number of items. Together, the value of these items may be material, but individually the value typically is neither material nor easy to forecast with high accuracy.

Once major cash flows have been scheduled, the distribution method can be used to forecast the approximate amounts of cash flows. Tracking historical cash flows to determine seasonal variations or day-of-the-week effects may prove useful, as historical information often is extremely accurate. However, if major changes are occurring in the organization's business or cash flows, historical information may have less validity for forecasting purposes.

Statistical Analysis   Statistical analysis can also be used for forecasting cash flows. Simple regression analysis attempts to create a formula that explains the causal relationship between a particular occurrence (an independent variable) and the resultant cash flows, which are considered to be dependent variables. Several factors can be modeled using multiple regression analysis.

Simple and multiple regression analysis can be done quickly in a spreadsheet or in specialized financial software. It is important to

Cash Flow Forecasting

In some industries, cash flows are significantly affected by local events, weather patterns, timing of holidays, and other similar issues. These may significantly affect customer sales, purchases, or check clearings, for example. Historical data may assist in uncovering these patterns.

One organization that issues large numbers of relatively small-value check payments found that local weather played the most significant role in check clearings. When short periods of very cold or inclement weather occurred, check clearings were down significantly, only to return to normal as the cold receded. During bad weather, check recipients put off depositing their checks until better weather returned. This was useful information since these payments represented the bulk of the organization's cash outflows.

understand the importance of the data used in the analysis, as well as its limitations. Some intelligence must be used in choosing factors that likely do affect cash flows.

Regression analysis creates a formula that describes the relationship between the two (using a "line of best fit"). It can appear to demonstrate a cause–and–effect relationship even when there is no such relationship. The R–squared statistic provides an indication of the strength of the relationship between the occurrence (independent variable) and resultant cash flows.

For example, suppose a treasury analyst models the impact of the day of the week on customer cash sales. The analyst finds that

IN THE REAL WORLD

Notable Quote

"Payment and settlement systems are to economic activity what roads are to traffic—necessary but typically taken for granted unless they cause an accident or bottlenecks to develop."

Source: Bank for International Settlements, Bank for International Settlements Annual Report 1994, *www.bis.org*.

Mondays and Fridays have higher sales, on average, than the remaining days of the week. Regression analysis will assist in defining the relationship between the day of the week and the cash flows from sales, based on historic data.

However, cash flows are subject to many external influences, and cash flow patterns can change over time. Therefore, regression analysis may not provide a complete picture of cash flows. It is necessary to apply intelligence and experience in the application of any statistical results and monitor the business environment to ensure that key factors have not changed.

Reconciliation

Although cash flow forecasts provide a view of expected cash flows, reconciliations permit treasury to compare transactions that were expected with transactions that actually occurred. A reconciliation adjusts for those items that differ from the forecast, both those that have unexpectedly cleared the account and those that unexpectedly have not cleared the account. Reconciliation is done on both cash flow amount and cash flow date.

TIPS & TECHNIQUES

Designing a Cash Flow Forecast

There are several considerations when designing or improving a cash flow forecast. These questions may be useful in determining an approach to forecasting and the attributes of the cash flow forecast:

- Who are the intended users of the forecast?

- How much detail and what kind of time horizon do the forecast users require?

- How often will the forecast be updated (daily, intraday, weekly, etc.)?

- If intraday updating is planned, how will the forecast users know that the cash forecast has been updated and is complete?

- Where will the data for the cash flow forecast come from?

- Can the cash flow forecast be integrated with other systems to support downloading of forecast data?

- Can the cash flow forecast be reformatted for different users?

- Can the cash flow forecast use historical data for statistical and other analysis?

- Can the forecast be maintained by a backup employee who may not have the same breadth of experience as the regular forecaster?

- Will the cash flow forecast include foreign currencies that have cash flows?

Reconciling should be done on a daily basis, so that errors and fraudulent items can be identified immediately. This also assists in ensuring the cash balance is as accurate as possible.

Although increasingly financial transactions move through accounts intraday, transactions can occur or be posted to an account any time during the 24-hour day. As a result, the most complete accounting of transactions typically is available the next business day. Previous day transactions are reported on the current day, while current-day transactions will be reported on the next business day. As a result, before any current-day forecasting can occur, it is necessary to adjust the current day's opening balance by any unexpected items that occurred on the previous day.

Variations on cash flow reporting can occur where items can be backdated, but these are normally exceptions. Backdating is a process by a financial institution to date a transaction as though it had occurred at a previous date, typically used to rectify errors.

The process of determining the opening balance in a bank account with daily balance and transaction reporting is similar to these seven steps. However, although the process is similar, the specific steps depend on the bank and technology services being used and the organization:

Step 1   Start with the expected closing position previous day from the cash flow forecast.

Step 2   Add previous day's bank data for prior day balances and float values (if provided).

Step 3   If automated reconciliation or matching is used, reconcile for unmatched transactions; otherwise, reconcile actual to forecasted transactions:

a. Adjust current-day forecast for cash inflows or cash out-flows that occurred but were not expected to occur (on the previous day).

b. Adjust current-day forecast for cash inflows or outflows that did not occur but were expected to occur (on the previous day).

c. Investigate any items that require further analysis.

Step 4 This should now have resulted in a cash position that is reconciled with the closing cash position reported by the bank.

Step 5 For accounts that provide availability float, update float to determine opening available cash position for the current day.

Step 6 Ensure any items that did not occur are placed back into the forecast if they are still likely to occur.

Step 7 Repeat for each account being reconciled.

The result of these steps is an expected balance prior to adding any of the current-day transactions, such as new investments or foreign exchange transactions. The current day's closing balance will not be known with certainty until all transaction information that cleared the account is received. When this process occurs overnight, the information typically will not be available to treasury until the next business day when the forecasting process begins again.

Reconciliation is one of the most commonly automated procedures if organizations use treasury software and electronic bank and transaction services. An automated matching can be done based on specific identifying criteria, leaving only exception items to be adjusted manually.

Given the preponderance of payment and check fraud, it is important that any automated reconciliation provide adequate matching to ensure that fraudulent items are not making it through. For example, when matching is done only on amount, items where the payee has changed will not be captured.

Foreign Currency Cash Forecasts

Organizations with foreign currency cash flows may find that maintaining cash forecasts for each currency can assist in identifying currency exposures and timing gaps where funding or investing may be necessary. Ideally, the forecast format allows the user to view the forecast by currency or from a consolidated cash flow view. When cash flows are consolidated across currencies, it is necessary for a conversion rate to be used to convert all currencies to a common currency, typically the main operating currency, such as U.S. dollars or euros.

The forecast format should enable the user to easily determine a balance for each currency in which there are cash flows and determine whether there is a cumulative deficit or excess of each currency over time based on reasonably certain cash flows. Short-term differences between currency inflows and currency outflows may offset over longer periods, so the cumulative totals by month, by quarter, or on an annual basis are also useful. Cash flows that offset over time represent a timing issue and are often managed using foreign exchange swaps. These are discussed with an example in Chapter 3. Cumulative gaps between cash inflows and outflows may require hedging.

A cash flow forecast for foreign currencies should be structured to recognize the timing delays in requesting payments or receiving notice of funds received. There is often a day or more delay, since foreign

TIPS & TECHNIQUES

Improving Cash Forecasts

Although senior management and decision makers consider accurate cash flow forecasts to be one of the most important contributions of treasury, forecasts are often inaccurate or information is not provided in a timely manner. In many cases, an improvement of relationships between disparate parts of an organization with cash flow information can assist in forecasting.

Cash flow information typically depends on people located in widespread parts of an organization. The importance of accurate and timely cash flow information must be transmitted to these individuals in order to obtain compliance. Presentations or memos, along with follow-up on missed items, may help. Some treasury professionals refer to the formal and informal "information network" that provides key data from individuals who see it coming.

Finally, improvements in cash forecasting can be achieved by changing the methods used for paying and receiving funds. Although the benefits of float are attractive, so is the ability to accurately forecast cash flows and make use of all excess cash. Float is discussed in more detail elsewhere in this chapter.

currency payments require a bank in the foreign currency jurisdiction to initiate the payment. Therefore, it is important to begin planning prior to the day that a cash flow is required.

Cash Receipts and Disbursements

Both cash receipts and disbursements involve payments, and the business of payments is evolving quickly. Common payment methods include checks, ACH (automated clearinghouse), and electronic payments. Other than cash and checks, almost all other payments are electronic, since they are recorded and maintained with information technology.

Although the use of checks is still significant, electronic forms of payment are increasing in importance. A study conducted by the Federal Reserve found that most U.S. noncash payments made in 2003 were electronic payments, a shift from 2000 when most non-cash payments were made by check.[1] In some countries, checks are rarely used.

New areas of growth include mobile payments, an electronic payment that is initiated through a mobile phone. Considering the number of mobile phones in use as of 2005 (almost 1 billion worldwide), such payments may offer significant opportunities.

IN THE REAL WORLD

Online Banking

The delivery of bank services and interfaces via the Internet is a relatively new phenomenon. Online banking systems function in a similar way to proprietary treasury workstations. Users can send their payment data to a financial institution via the Internet, where payments are made in the chosen format (e.g., paper or electronic). For obvious reasons, significant security issues exist. Although financial institutions and standard-setting organizations are working hard to ensure security, it remains an ongoing issue for many treasurers. Online banking systems may provide services and alternatives for both large and smaller organizations or for those organizations that do not have large budgets for treasury infrastructure.

Float

Float describes the time that funds spend in transition between stages in the payment cycle due to typical time delays between the stages. Float is most easily described through an example of a check used to pay an outstanding invoice.

Mail float is the time that elapses between the mailing of a check and its receipt by the recipient. When a payor writes and mails a check, it must be delivered from the payor's point of mailing to the recipient's or payee's address, whether an office or a lockbox. The time that it takes for this to occur is considered mail float, and it is to the advantage of the payor (provided that interest is not accruing to the detriment of the payor). The location of the check mailing point and its recipient's location clearly affect how quickly a check is received, and thus impacts mail float since some locations are able to receive mail and have outbound mail picked up more quickly than others. The longer funds remain in the payor's account, the better.

When the recipient receives the check, it must be processed. Processing float is the time between the receipt of a check by the recipient and its deposit into a financial institution. The envelope containing the check is opened, the supporting documentation is checked, and the check begins to be processed through accounts receivable and eventually to be deposited at the company's financial institution.

When checks received are not processed and deposited in a timely manner, processing float can represent a cost to the organization. Processing float is controlled by the efficiency of the recipient organization and its internal processes. If employees are slow to

continued on next page

process the check, or if time sensitivity of the process is not respected, days can be lost to processing float. The length of time this takes is also to the benefit of the payor, because it slows the check from clearing the account, but it is also to the detriment of the recipient, who has unutilized funds sitting in paper checks.

From the perspective of the recipient, once the check has been deposited into the recipient's account, there may be a delay in the availability of funds. Availability float is the time that elapses from the deposit of a check by the recipient until the funds are made available to the check recipient. Determined by the receiving financial institution, availability float can vary up to several days, although normally it is zero to two days, depending on the financial institution, its relationship with the depositor, clearing times, and other factors. Availability float is not a universal concept. For example, except in unusual circumstances, there is no availability float in Canada.

From the perspective of the payor, in addition to mail and processing float, additional float may arise as a result of a delay in the financial institution's debiting of the payor's account, despite the deposit of the check by the recipient. This is known as clearing float, and it is the time, if any, between the deposit of the check and the debit of funds from the payor.

The importance of float to an individual organization depends on the dollar amounts in float and the opportunity cost of money.

Checks

In many countries, including the United States, checks remain a popular method of payment. Checks have many advantages. They are convenient, provide a paper trail, slow the speed of disbursements for payors, are widely accepted in the business world, and can be used cheaply, with few fees or setup charges. Due to the fact that almost every recipient, business or consumer, can accept checks, they remain very popular. A study by the U.S. Federal Reserve found that 36.7 billion check payments were made in 2003, a decline from 2000 but still a sizable number.[2]

In the United States, checks are cleared through one of four major methods:

1. Check clearing through the Federal Reserve clearing service

2. Check clearing directly between individual banks (known as direct sends)

3. Check clearing that involves checks both written on and deposited to accounts with the same bank (known as on-us)

4. Clearinghouse check clearing, which exchange checks drawn on clearinghouse members, with final settlement by debit or credit to the banks' Federal Reserve accounts

As a result of legal changes and lawsuits, there is much more responsibility on the check payor today than in the past. Although estimates exist, most cases of fraud, even major fraud, go unreported, and it is estimated that the vast majority of such fraud is perpetrated internally by insiders. As a result, it is critical that organizations recognize their responsibilities and not make the assumption that the financial institution will rectify a potential fraud issue. Rules vary from country to country and are subject to change or legal challenge. It is the responsibility of cash and treasury management personnel to ensure that the maximum precautions available are taken.

Although checks are common, there are implicit costs in their widespread use, particularly the growing incidence of fraud. Fraud is

TIPS & TECHNIQUES

Positive Pay

The use of checks for disbursements creates risk through opportunities for fraud and error. Positive pay is a bank service designed to reduce the opportunities for check fraud. The issuing company sends a file to the bank with data on issued checks. As checks are presented for clearing, they are compared to the items sent to the bank by the issuer. Those that do not match are reported to the issuing company for decision. Payee match services are also available that permit matching on payee name as well as amount, date, and item number.

causing significant losses within the financial system for financial institutions and check users, not only in the United States but also in other countries. Initiatives such as Check 21 in the United States and TECP (Truncation and Electronic Presentment) in Canada are designed to reduce some of the risks associated with check payments.

Organizations using checks should ensure they have strong controls to protect against fraud. Use of electronic payments (which also require fraud prevention), positive pay, payee matching, control over check stock, check stock with security features, daily reconciliation by someone not responsible for the transactions, and strong internal controls are all common approaches. Concerns about fraud should be discussed with an experienced professional.

ACH System

Automated clearinghouse (ACH) payments are used for both business and retail payments as an electronic alternative to checks. Rules

IN THE REAL WORLD

Check Truncation

In the United States, the Check Clearing for the 21st Century Act (known as Check 21) permits check-clearing organizations to forward an electronic copy of the check, rather than the original paper copy, for processing and payment. The result is the creation of a substitute check that can be used as evidence and in the audit process. Check 21 is voluntary for U.S. financial institutions. However, significant cost savings through more streamlined processing of check clearing and reducing processing time are likely to make it commonplace in the future.

Although the concept of truncation is not new, the legislation to support Check 21 was hastened by the grounding of commercial aircraft in Canada and the United States following the 2001 terrorist attacks. It was introduced in 2004. A similar, though nonvoluntary, initiative is under way in Canada, known as Truncation and Electronic Presentment (TECP).

In the United States, ARC (conversion of accounts receivable entries) can be used to convert consumer checks into electronic form. Consumer checks are often sent to an accounts receivable location, such as a lockbox. There they can be converted to ACH debits, provided that prior notice has been given to the consumer payor.

and standards are governed by the Electronic Payments Association (NACHA). Such payments are designed for use with low-value, high-volume transactions.

ACH payments provide reduced costs of payment, increase control over when a payment is made, and eliminate mail and processing delays. An ACH payment is initiated as a debit or credit from the originator to the receiver. Both debit and credit occur the same day, also eliminating float issues. As a result, they may improve forecasting accuracy.

ACH electronic depository transfers (EDTs) are ACH transactions used for funds concentration. If the need for funds can be established with one or two days' lead time, an ACH may be used as a cheaper alternative to a Fedwire transfer, a more expensive payment option discussed in the next section.

The Federal Reserve is the largest operator of automated clearinghouse payments in the United States. In 2004, more than 6 billion commercial interbank ACH transactions were processed through the Fed's ACH system, compared with 1.7 billion a decade earlier. The Electronic Payments Network (*www.epaynetwork.com*), a private ACH processor, also provides ACH payments and services. The biggest NACHA-volume financial institutions include JPMorgan, Bank of America, Wells Fargo, Wachovia, and Citigroup.[3]

The biggest use of ACH payments is for direct payroll deposit, but ACH is also used for business payments, federal tax withholding payments, and many other, primarily routine, transactions. In addition, ACH debits can be initiated by consumers over the Internet for making payments.

FedACH international payments are electronic credit transactions initiated by U.S. depository institutions for bank-to-bank transfers. Canada, Mexico, and several European countries (Austria, Germany, the Netherlands, Switzerland, and United Kingdom) are participating.

It is necessary to take fraud prevention precautions for all forms of payment including ACH payments. ACH debit fraud prevention tools include the use of debit blocks on accounts used for ACH transactions, bank filtering tools, positive pay, check blocking, and daily reconciliation by someone not responsible for the transactions to uncover unauthorized items. Separation of accounts used for checks and electronic payments, as well as separate accounts for ACH debits and credits, may also help.

Electronic payments are also potential areas for fraud, and some major events have occurred. In many cases, the fraud was perpetrated as a result of gaining access to the system that permitted an electronic transfer to occur. The use of strong internal controls, passwords, restricted access, and restricted authorization to prevent access to funds transfer initiation systems should be used. Concerns about fraud always should be discussed with an experienced professional.

High-Value Electronic Payments

Large-value systems differ from retail payment systems. Although a high-value payment system can be used to make a small-value payment, cost and ease of transaction are factors that necessarily influence the decision about which method to use.

Large-value systems differ from retail payment systems because they are important to the broader financial community. They are systematically important, meaning their failure can threaten financial market stability. If a financial institution were to default on a settlement obligation, it could affect many other financial institutions. As a result, great efforts have gone into developing the various high-value systems that are in use globally.

In the United States, two systems facilitate high-value payments. The Fedwire system is operated by the Federal Reserve, and it processes electronic large-value items with same-day value and finality of settlement. The Fedwire system is a real-time gross settlement system that is used for domestic U.S. dollar payments, typically those of high value.

The Clearing House Interbank Payments System (CHIPS) is operated by the Clearing House Payments Company, which is privately owned by a number of major financial institutions. CHIPS processes more than US$1.3 trillion in about 260,000 transactions on an average day, the majority resulting from settlement of foreign exchange and Eurodollar trades. CHIPS uses bilateral and multilateral netting to settle payments in real time. The CHIPS system is unique in high-value systems because it can transmit large amounts of remittance information along with payments.

Canadian domestic high-value payments use the Large Value Transfer System (LVTS) operated by the Canadian Payments Association. The LVTS is a real-time settlement system that provides Canadian dollar payments that are final and irrevocable. There is a C$25 million cap on the value of payments made by check or bank draft. Larger amounts must use the LVTS.

The Trans-European Automated Real-time Gross Settlement Express Transfer (TARGET) system for high-value euro payments is an interlinking real-time system that connects the domestic real-time gross settlement systems of 15 European countries. These payment systems include those of the 12 euro countries, plus Denmark, Sweden, and the United Kingdom. TARGET is operated by the individual countries' central banks and the European Central Bank. TARGET payments are immediate and final. An improved system, TARGET2, is planned for 2007.

Europe also has Euro1, a multilateral net settlement system that conducts credit transfers and direct debits. These payments are processed during the business day and balances are settled at the end of the day through the European Central Bank.

Other Payment Methods

Other methods for disbursements include imprest accounts that are funded periodically at a particular balance for a specific purpose, multiple drawee checks that can be presented at a bank other than the bank on which they are drawn, and payable-through drafts that are drawn on the payor rather than the payor's bank.

Debit cards and credit cards have become increasingly popular methods of payment. A study by the U.S. Federal Reserve found that increases in transactions involving debit cards accounted for half of all the growth in electronic payments from 2000 to 2003.[4] In 2003, there were 15.6 billion debit card transactions, almost double the number in 2000.

Purchasing cards reduce the cost of purchasing for small items and amounts. There is significant cost associated with purchasing small items using purchase orders, receiving, and invoicing. Purchase cards, which should have systems in place to reduce opportunities for misuse, cost a fraction of the purchase order method.

Cash Aggregation

Cash aggregation is the collection and utilization of cash as quickly as possible. Depending on the financial institution and the country in which an organization operates, cash aggregation services can assist in managing dispersed cash pools for use at a central location. This may help to improve returns on excess cash balances or make cash available for debt reduction.

Wire Payment Checklist

This wire payment checklist of information should be provided by the sending organization in order to ensure timely delivery of funds via wire transfer:

- Name, address, and account number of sender

- Name and account number of recipient

- Recipient's financial institution

- Branch number (transit number) of recipient's financial institution (the branch where the account is actually held)

- Amount of payment

- Payment value date

- Information regarding the details of the remittance, such as invoices paid or reference numbers

For recipients of wire transfers, several steps should be taken, including:

- A discussion should be initiated with the organization's financial institution prior to receiving transfers, if possible.

- Ensure that the financial institution has specific instructions as to notifying the organization about incoming funds and how remittance information included with the funds transfer is to be treated.

- The recipient should also ensure that the sender has complete information, including correct corporate or organizational name, name of the receiving financial institution, account number, and transit or branch number.

Source: Canadian Payments Association, *www.cdnpay.ca.*

Organizations that operate branch and subsidiary operations may find that each requires one or more bank accounts. Typically, there is a need for funds in those accounts, even if the amounts are small, to cover unexpected payments or requirements. Organizations with many operations and bank accounts may find that significant funds are tied up in these balances and could be better utilized through centralization.

Cash aggregation services may simplify account administration and control. Although there are others, some of the most common tools to assist with cash aggregation include zero-balance accounts, controlled disbursement accounts, and pooling.

Zero-Balance Account

A zero-balance account (ZBA) automatically moves funds from individual accounts within the same financial institution to a master concentration account on a regular, typically daily, basis. While the individual accounts may be used for cash collection or disbursements (e.g., payroll), the master concentration account is used to collect and utilize excess funds from the individual accounts within the structure.

The ZBA is a disbursement account on which checks can be written. As checks are cleared against the account, an automated transfer of funds occurs from the master account to cover them.

With zero balancing, individual positive account balances are reduced to zero (or to another predetermined balance), while accounts in deficit are increased to zero or other balance. Funds transfers actually occur, and as a result there are legal and tax considerations depending on the corporate or organizational structure. In addition, there may be explicit costs associated with the funds transfers and implicit costs to manage and reconcile.

Zero balancing has the benefit of providing access to organizational cash funds that can then be deployed for the best available return—paying down debt or payment against a line of credit, for example.

Controlled Disbursement

Controlled disbursement is a service used specifically for cash disbursements. Each morning, banks provide their controlled disbursement customers with information about checks to be presented that day, allowing customers to forecast with accuracy the check clearings to occur and the necessary funding that is required for the account.

Participating U.S. banks offer controlled disbursement accounts that are funded once per day. The funding covers all the checks to be cleared on that business day. Those banks that are part of the High Dollar Sort Group program will receive a second presentment and therefore provide a second update to bank customers using controlled disbursement services.

Pooling

Pooling refers to bank services that aggregate cash from various bank accounts, either on a notional or actual basis. To facilitate pooling, credit facilities may need to be arranged to cover debit balances within in the pooled accounts.

Pooling is common in Europe where many crossborder transactions utilize the same currency due to the introduction of the euro. Pooling is relatively straightforward within one country, although legal rules may still restrict its use. However, transborder pooling is more complex, as countries' individual legal and tax rules may limit or prohibit certain aspects of pooling. Some countries prohibit pooling altogether.

The ability to do physical versus notional pooling depends on local country regulations and corporate legal structure. Physical pooling means that funds are actually moved from pooling accounts into the central account. Notional pooling means that funds are not actually transferred, but balance and transaction data are reported as if transfers had taken place. In addition, interest is calculated as if transfers had occurred.

The term pooling is also used to refer to an organizational strategy where a central treasury acts as an in-house bank to other parts of the organization.

Some countries prohibit or restrict intercompany transactions, including cash pooling. As a result, expert assistance is necessary in this area, since tax and legal issues should be determined prior to engaging in such transactions.

Lockboxes

Lockboxes are locations where payments, particularly checks, are collected. Lockboxes provide a number of advantages for receiving payments, including faster processing of receipts, potential for reduced float, and the reporting done by the lockbox provider. There are two major types of lockboxes.

Wholesale lockboxes are used for business-to-business payments. Retail lockboxes are used for consumer payments with high volumes but smaller dollar amounts. Due to their higher volumes, they typically have more rigorous processing requirements. Hybrid lockboxes with attributes of each also exist.

Global Cash Management

Global cash management adds a layer of complexity to the cash management process. In addition to the issues of forecasting, control, and liquidity, legal and regulatory issues may affect an organization's cash management. At present, a handful of major financial institutions dominate the global cash management business, handling the bulk of global regional and global cash management.

There are a number of techniques and bank services for consolidating and managing cash between accounts, financial institutions, both domestically and cross border. However, even in jurisdictions with a common currency, such as the euro zone, there can be difficulties consolidating cash seamlessly. Cross-border transactions, even in the same currency, may have legal, regulatory, or tax implications. Such transactions, therefore, require the expertise of a professional who is well versed in the country and cross-border specifics.

One major consideration with global cash management is in the area of electronic payments. In addition to the vast differences between countries, in many countries, checks are not widely used, and in some countries, they are almost nonexistent. For example, many European countries have a very high level of maturity with electronic payments. Although national automated clearinghouse payment systems exist, the trend appears to be toward international payments linkages.

Pooling is a technique to notionally or physically aggregate cash between different parts of an organization. Excess funds can be used to offset a deficit in other accounts. On a daily basis, positive and negative balances are aggregated, and interest earned or due is calculated.

IN THE REAL WORLD

Clearing and Settlement

Clearing is the process of transmitting, reconciling, and, in some cases, confirming payment orders prior to settlement. It can also include the netting instructions (the offsetting of several positions or obligations between trading partners or participants) and the establishment of final positions for settlement. Settlement is the discharging of obligations related to payment transactions between two or more parties.

Source: ECB Issues Paper for ECB Conference, held November 10, 2004, "E-Payments without Frontiers." Original source: ECB Blue Book, *Payment and Securities Settlement Systems in the EU,* 3rd ed., June 2001.

Typically, accounts are at the same bank and credit facilities may be required. Although intuitively appealing, pooling can present logistical complexities due to legal and regulatory environments in other countries.

Zero balancing, which is commonly used in the United States, can also be used in global cash management. In a zero-balancing arrangement, accounts with excess funds are used to fund accounts with a deficit, provided that accounts are within the same bank and country. Subsidiaries use their own accounts, and transfers into and out of the master account fund them.

Cash Management Checklist

Many activities can be used to improve cash management practices. The following practices are often useful:

Receipts and Disbursement-Related Practices

- Cash collected as quickly as possible
- Disbursement payments delayed as long as possible without violating supplier and vendor relationships

Staff-Related Practices

- Comprehensive controls to protect cash assets and payments from theft and fraudulent activity
- Knowledgeable, well-rounded staff
- Clear division of duties
- Appropriate compensation structure

Cash Flow Forecasting Practices

- Cash forecast regularly updated
- Cash forecast rolling forward
- Automation of regular cash flow forecast items such as payroll, lease payments, and so forth
- Automation of routine processes, such as downloads of bank balance and transaction data
- Ad hoc management reporting
- Information available based on different criteria and detail
- Different views of cash flow data

Management Practices

- Integrated view of cash management across the organization

IN THE REAL WORLD

Cash Management in Canada

Canadian cash management is simplified considerably in that most domestic funds deposited have same-day availability—there is no availability float. Canadian check (known as cheque) processing is facilitated by a small number of large banks with extensive branch networks and processing facilities. Most payments processing is done by Symcor and Intria Items Inc. Lockboxes are used only for high-volume payment recipients. The Automated Clearing and Settlements System (ACSS) handles check clearing, and the Large Value Transfer System (LVTS) handles large-value items. The payments system and the associated rules are managed by the Canadian Payments Association.

Source: Canadian Payments Association, *www.cdnpay.ca.*

- Timely and accurate information from other parts of the organization that affect cash flows
- Involvement of accounting, audit, and legal professionals
- Clear audit trail

Summary

- Cash management is a key component of treasury. Cash is essential to the long-run survival of an organization, and it must be protected from theft, error, and mismanagement.
- Cash management includes cash flow forecasting, which is a critical activity for an organization.

- A good understanding of the importance of cash management by others in an organization will help to make it as
  efficient as possible.

Notes

1. The 2004 Federal Reserve Payment Study, "Analysis of Noncash
   Payment Trends in the United States: 2000-2003." Federal Reserve.
2. Ibid.
3. "NACHA Top 50-Volumes for Year 2004," *www.nacha.org.*
4. Ibid. note 1.

CHAPTER 3

Liquidity Management

After reading this chapter, you should be able to:

- Develop strategies for managing liquidity.
- Identify attributes of money market securities.
- Evaluate alternatives for managing short-term investment portfolios and financing short-term cash requirements.

Introduction

Liquidity is the ability of an organization to meet its short-term financial obligations. Successful organizations must maintain a balance between underutilized cash balances and adequate short-term resources to conduct day-to-day operations. These are some of the challenges of liquidity management.

Liquidity management encompasses the management of cash balances, including short-term funding and investments for excess cash.

The alternatives for raising cash during temporary shortages and the opportunities to invest excess cash on a short-term basis are important to the functioning of an organization.

Liquidity is important for several reasons, including:

- Providing the ability to take advantage of opportunities as they arise, for new products, acquisitions, or timely investments, for example

- Funding for future projects and acquisitions

- Serving as a financial buffer against an unexpected decline in revenues or sales

- Meeting the need for collateral against borrowing or debt issuance

- Funding cash-intensive activities, such as research and development

One of the critical treasury roles is the management of cash balances. If there is excess cash, funds can be moved into an interest-earning account overnight, or they can be invested for a longer period of time. The focus with short-term assets is on risk, return, and liquidity.

Although cash management focuses on the methods used to make and receive payments, liquidity management focuses on the balances that arise as a result of those transactions. It is also closely associated with management of working capital, which includes accounts payable and accounts receivable and ultimately affects liquidity. Anything that affects the ability of the organization to fund short-term obligations is potentially within the scope of liquidity management.

There are a number of methods to measure the effectiveness of liquidity management, including availability of liquidity, working capital ratios, accounts receivables outstanding, and average cash balances, for example. Related issues to consider include bank charges and costs of funding.

Money Market

Many organizations manage excess liquidity in the form of cash and short-term assets in the money market. The money market is the wholesale market for cash, liabilities, and short-term fixed income securities. It facilitates short-term investing of excess cash and short-term funding for borrowers.

The money market is mostly an institutional market, with amounts ranging from about $100,000 to many millions. Maturity of most money market instruments is typically from overnight (one day) to about a year, although longer-term securities may also be used.

Money market investments typically meet these attributes:

- Relatively short term to maturity

- Low-risk, high-credit quality

- Liquidity requirements vary depending on the investor; however, the requirement is usually for high liquidity

Money market securities are subject to market risk, primarily interest rate risk, foreign exchange risk if they are foreign currency denominated securities, and credit risk. These risks are discussed in more detail in Chapter 6.

Commonly used financial instruments for managing excess short-term cash include bank deposits, bankers' acceptances, certificates of deposit, commercial paper, Treasury bills and other government securities, and money market mutual or pooled funds.

IN THE REAL WORLD

Monetary Policy

The U.S. Federal Reserve sets monetary policy in the United States through the Federal Open Market Committee (FOMC). Open market operations, which are used to manage short-term interest rates, are conducted mostly through repurchase agreements (repos, or sale and repurchase agreements) and the purchase and sale of government securities.

The Bank of Canada affects monetary policy primarily through the overnight rate charged between money market dealers. The Bank maintains the overnight rate within a 50 basis point (1/2 percent) band, with the upper band known as the Bank Rate. The target for the overnight rate is the midpoint between the upper and lower bands. The Bank lends at the Bank Rate and pays the bottom of the band on surplus balances for participants in the Large Value Transfer System (LVTS). The LVTS system for high-value payments is discussed in more detail in Chapter 2. The Bank of Canada also uses repos and reverse repos (reverse repurchase agreements, or the purchase and re-sale of securities) to conduct its open market operations whenever the overnight rate moves too far from the target rate.

Participants

The money market is, for the most part, a dealer market. Dealers trade among themselves and with customers in a virtual dealer marketplace. Participants in the money market include banks and other financial institutions, investment dealers, governments, fund managers, insurance companies, and corporations, as well as central banks. Trading may be facilitated by interdealer firms that intermediate transactions between dealers at financial institutions for wholesale amounts. Increasingly, electronic marketplaces facilitate trading in money market securities.

Financial institutions, particularly large banks, are active participants in the money market because of their significant cash management requirements that arise as a result of their core business and financial market activities. Smaller financial institutions may focus on liquidity and interest rate risk management, while larger financial institutions employ money market traders for proprietary and customer trading within specific areas of expertise. In large trading rooms, money market traders specialize in particular markets or instruments, such as government debt (e.g., Treasury bills) and short-term corporate debt (e.g., commercial paper), foreign exchange, and various types of derivatives.

Governments and their agencies incur obligations at various levels of government from the federal level down to the municipal level, and they issue debt to support their activities and finance both short- and long-term shortfalls. Governments may be both issuers of and investors in money market securities.

Corporations make up the last major tier of money market participants, both as issuers and as investors. Although some corporations are small money market investors, others are extremely large and sophisticated, and their portfolios may rival those of some financial institutions. Corporations may use the services of financial institutions to bundle and package assets for security creation, such as the securitization market. In addition, corporations issue their own obligations through debt issues.

Money Market Basics

Money market securities are fixed income securities with short-term maturities. As such, they provide contractual payments in the form of interest (periodically or at maturity) and return of principal to investors. Most money market securities mature in under one year, although the investment universe may include securities of slightly longer maturity and some, such as mutual funds, have no maturity date.

Nominal interest rates consist of a lending rate for money, plus an inflation component and a credit component. Because most money market securities are relatively short term in nature, inflation is less an issue than credit. The quality of investment depends on the likelihood of repayment and therefore the creditworthiness of the issuer. The higher the credit rating, all else being equal, the lower the yield. The downgrading or otherwise altering of an issuer's credit rating can have a significant effect on its ability to sell debt securities.

Most money market securities pay interest at maturity. A few have periodic interest payments, either because they mature in more than one year or because the original issue had coupon payments.

Money market instruments are either discount or interest bearing. Discount instruments are sold at discount and mature at their par or face value. The difference is interest income to the investor.

Interest-bearing instruments are similar in nature to a bank deposit, where a face or par amount is invested and it earns income, which is paid at maturity. Money market instruments generally do not have coupon interest or periodic interest payments. Instead, interest is usually paid at maturity, and most instruments mature in under one year.

Most money market trading is for same-day settlement, although the specifics vary by country and sometimes instrument. Next-day trading is also available. Fixed income securities with longer original terms to maturity may settle three business days after the trade date

(T+3). Initiatives to reduce settlement time for fixed income and equity securities from T+3 to T+1 have been sidelined as of the present.

Money market dealers and customers are linked by telephone and electronic dealing systems. A basic trading protocol exists in the money market as well as in other types of trading. When two-sided (bid and offer) prices are given, the dealer making the price (price maker) has the right to the favorable price or rate. In the money market, where price and interest rate are inversely related, this means the price taker (the dealer requesting a price) borrows at the higher rate (lower price) and invests at the lower interest rate (higher price). This protocol exists when banks and dealers trade with one another, as well as when they trade with their customers.

Government Securities

In the United States, the most common government securities are Treasury bills, which are discount obligations issued by the U.S. Treasury. These short-term federal government obligations traditionally offer the lowest return and are considered to be very low risk. They are issued through an auction process weekly, with regular maturities.

Securities issued by a government agency include bonds issued by Federal National Mortgage Association (FNMA, or commonly known as Fannie Mae), Government National Mortgage Association (GNMA, or commonly known as Ginnie Mae). Although generally grouped with government securities, these agency securities are not explicitly guaranteed by the U.S. government. Municipal bonds are issued by city and community governments in two types: general obligation bonds and revenue bonds.

The most common government securities in Canada are also Treasury bills, which are discounted obligations issued by the Government of Canada that trade on yield. As with U.S. Treasury bills, they are considered to be top credit quality and very low risk and are issued through a regular auction process. Treasury bills are also issued by some provincial governments, and their credit quality and liquidity are slightly below the federal issues. Other securities are issued by or guaranteed by a number of Canadian government agencies.

Certificates of Deposit

Certificates of deposit (CDs) are interest bearing and may be negotiable or nonnegotiable. Most money market CDs are negotiable and traded in the secondary market. There are several types:

- *Fixed rate CDs.* Interest rate is set for term of the CD; may pay periodic interest if maturity is greater than one year.

- *Variable rate CDs.* Interest rate is reset on a predetermined frequency, for example, monthly or quarterly.

- *Eurodollar CDs.* Issued by financial institutions outside the United States in U.S. dollars.

- *Yankee CDs.* Issued in U.S. dollars by foreign banks operating in the United States.

Commercial Paper

The most common corporate money market securities are commercial paper issues, which are unsecured debt of corporations. The companies issuing commercial paper are normally relatively well known to the investor community. Most commercial paper matures in 30 days

TIPS & TECHNIQUES

The Eurocurrency Market

Not to be confused with the euro, the currency adopted by a dozen European nations in economic union, the term Eurocurrency refers to currency deposits held by banks outside the country's borders.

For example, Eurodollars are dollar-denominated deposits held by a bank outside the United States. Similarly, Euroyen are yen deposits held by a bank outside Japan. However, the name is a bit of a misnomer. Although the bank holding the deposits is outside the country, the currency itself is placed on the bank's behalf with correspondent banks in the country. The traditional (and largest) market for Eurocurrencies is London. London is a geographically central location and a major center of trading activity.

or less and rarely has a term of more than 270 days to avoid Securities and Exchange Commission (SEC) registration in the US.[1]

Bankers' Acceptances

Bankers' acceptances (BAs) are issues of corporate debt that have been accepted (guaranteed) by a bank. The guarantee of the bank makes BAs popular with investors. BAs are created when a bank lends to a corporation, adding its own guarantee. The newly issued BA is then sold to investors.

For smaller amounts of debt, or issuance by companies whose names are not well known, the issuance of BAs is an alternative for raising short-term funds. BAs often are used in financing of import/export transactions. Although these securities originate as corporate debt, they are guaranteed ("accepted") by a financial institution and

IN THE REAL WORLD

Primary versus Secondary Market

Money market securities often are offered to investors through the wide distribution networks of investment dealers and financial institutions. Dealers can act as principals, buying the issue and selling it to earn a profit, or as agents. In addition, many issuers sell debt issues directly to their investor community, such as the direct commercial paper issuers.

When a money market security is issued initially, it is said to be a primary market transaction, as the security is created and sold initially. Each time the security is sold thereafter, it is said to be trading in the secondary market. Once the debt has been sold by the issuer, it trades in the secondary market, and it may be bought and sold dozens of times before its maturity.

become a liability of the financial institution. As a result, although they are originated through corporate indebtedness, they are properly classified as bank obligations and trade on the strength of the guaranteeing bank. In the United States, BAs are issued most often as a result of trade transactions.

Asset-Backed Securities

Asset-backed securities are a growing class of securities that often are created through securitization activities. In securitization, a pool of assets, such as consumer loans, are packaged together, along with additional credit enhancements, and sold to investors.

Asset-backed securities may be structured as trusts, and the investors receive returns that are generally slightly more attractive than other money market securities. Asset-backed securities are used to repackage auto loans, credit card receivables, and mortgages, among other things. It is important to assess the attributes of each issue, including credit enhancement techniques and legal issues.

Foreign Exchange Swaps

Foreign exchange swaps are commonly used for cash management purposes, particularly within large organizations that have cash management requirements in several currencies.

Due to the fact that foreign exchange is also a key business of financial institutions, trading in foreign exchange and foreign exchange swaps is common. Foreign exchange swaps, which are discussed in this chapter and in Chapter 4, provide the link between foreign exchange and money markets.

Not to be confused with longer-term currency and interest rate swaps, a foreign exchange swap consists of a spot transaction with a simultaneously arranged forward transaction. Currencies are exchanged at both the spot date and the forward date. Since the spot and forward rates are set at the time of the transaction, the difference between the two rates reflects the interest differential between the two currencies over the term of the swap. The result is the ability to use the foreign exchange markets to borrow and lend currencies, augmenting other money market transactions.

Three major types of foreign exchange swaps are used for cash management purposes, depending on the start date of the swap. Foreign exchange swaps may be transacted beginning the same day

---

TIPS & TECHNIQUES

Foreign Exchange Swap Example

A U.S. company has excess Canadian dollars that it does not need for six months, at which time it will use the Canadian dollars. In the meantime, it would like to invest the excess Canadian dollars temporarily and obtain the use of U.S. dollars, since most of its operating expenses are in U.S. dollars.

The company enters into a foreign exchange swap with its bank. For value spot, it buys U.S. dollars $5 million at 1.3500 CAD/USD and sells C$6,750,000. Simultaneously, for value six months from spot, it agrees to sell back the U.S. dollars $5,000,000 at 1.3595 CAD/USD and buy back C$6,797,500.

The difference between the spot rate and the forward rate of .0095 or 95 points is set at the time the swap is transacted. It is also the net interest rate differential between Canadian and U.S. dollars over the six months of the swap on US$5 million, or C$47,500. The positive difference is due to the fact that that the company is investing the currency with the higher interest rate.

As a result of the swap, the U.S. company has effectively invested its excess Canadian dollars for six months and gained U.S. dollars in the meantime. To assess the merit of the swap, its net cost or gain must be compared with other money market alternatives. The credit quality of the financial institution counterparty must also be assessed.

(cash value), the next business day or "tom-next" (local spot value), or two business days or "spot-next" (international spot value). Amounts normally must be wholesale amounts of at least $5 million or more, but much larger amounts are not uncommon. Foreign exchange issues are discussed in more detail in Chapter 4.

TIPS & TECHNIQUES

Canadian Money Market Securities

Canadian money market securities are similar in many respects to U.S. money market securities. Most are Canadian dollar discounted securities that trade on the basis of yield, which measures return given price, rather than discount rate, used to calculate the discount amount for certain instruments. Calculations are based on a 365-day year. Commonly used instruments include:

- Government of Canada Treasury bills, issued by the federal government

- Provincial government treasury bills, issued by the provincial governments

- Commercial paper, including asset-backed issues

- Bankers' acceptances (Schedule I or Schedule II, depending on the type of bank that provides the acceptance or guarantee)

Other Securities

The money market also contains securities with call or retraction features. Originally issued as longer-term securities, as their maturity approaches, they may become potential money market investments.

A callable security allows the issuer to retire the security at a predetermined call price and date. Call features are attractive to debt issuers because they enable the issuer to refinance at a lower interest rate, should interest rates decline. Normally a minimum holding period is provided for the investor before the security can be called away by the issuer. A fixed income instrument may have a call schedule consisting of several call dates and prices throughout its life. Generally, the earlier in its maturity it is called, the greater the call premium paid to the investor.

It is important to be aware of all the attributes of securities before they are selected for a portfolio, whether a money market or term portfolio. For callable securities, this would include the next call price and date, subsequent call prices and dates, and notice requirement. Knowing this will enable the investor to assess the likelihood of a call occurring and therefore the relative attractiveness of the security. Investors may choose callable securities despite being likely to be called, if their credit quality and yield to call is attractive compared with alternatives.

IN THE REAL WORLD

Sweep Accounts

Sweep accounts permit excess funds in U.S. corporate demand accounts to earn interest on overnight balances. They exist because of Federal Reserve Regulation Q, which prevents the paying of interest on corporate demand deposits. Funds within sweep accounts are moved (swept) out of the account at the end of each business day into an interest-earning account. Although the rate of return may be lower than that otherwise available in the money market, it is a viable alternative to funds that otherwise would not be utilized.

The term "sweep" also has another meaning: It sometimes is used to describe the aggregation of cash from many accounts into a single account in global cash management. This is discussed in more detail in Chapter 2.

Other securities include retractable securities and those with periodic interest rate resets.

Money Market Mutual or Pooled Funds

Mutual or pooled funds are portfolios of securities in which investors hold units or shares. Normally these units fluctuate with the net asset value of the underlying assets, but many funds holding money market securities set the net asset value at a fixed (but not guaranteed) net asset value. Money market funds are popular with money market investors because of their convenience.

One of the advantages to mutual funds is that reporting, management, and analysis are also outsourced. Many funds offer excellent liquidity, although some planning and cash flow forecasting is necessary. In addition, funds may offer attractive cutoff times for new money, which may enable treasury to complete the day's transactions before rolling excess cash into a fund.

The organization using money market funds should ensure that the funds are managed in a style that is appropriate for the investing organization. Considerations include the investment style, types of limits employed such as credit limits, whether leverage is utilized, and whether securities lending is used. It is also necessary to assess what access to funds exists under volatile market conditions. Fund managers may be able to defer redemptions under such conditions.

Short-term Investment Management

The existence of a short-term money market portfolio offers several advantages to the organization, including:

- Meeting the need for liquidity within the organization to take advantage of opportunities as they arise, or to fund future specific projects or acquisitions, for example

- Providing an opportunity to earn investment income; even with relatively low interest rates, this can be significant in a large organization

- Creating a buffer against more risky business activities, as may be the case during the early or growth phase of a company

- Meeting the need for collateral, if any, for future borrowing or financing activities

Money market investment management can be undertaken using an active or passive approach. The decision depends on the type of organization, management's intentions, internal policies, the financial management team, and the portfolio itself, including size, composition, purpose, and so on.

An actively managed money market portfolio attempts to create additional returns for the organization. However, in attempting to outperform, the portfolio will incur additional risk that may result in poorer than average results. Management must be comfortable with the increased risk that results from an increased performance objective.

More passive approaches to cash management may result in something similar to the market rate of return, less management costs. A passive portfolio management strategy attempts to track a benchmark rate of return, looking for protection against adverse market movements rather than trying to outperform the overall trend of the market. Passive portfolio management techniques, because they utilize strategies that are not attempting to outperform the market, typically involve lower levels of risk.

Regardless of the type of investment management strategy pursued, money market assets are valuable to the organization. Their management should be outlined in an investment policy and the ramifications of the investment style understood and formally sanctioned by senior management and the board of directors.

Passive Techniques

The most common passive techniques for short-term investment management are creating a maturity ladder and matching. Both are relatively low analysis and low cost, because no interest rate forecasting is involved. However, even with relatively passive investment management techniques, credit analysis is still an ongoing critical part of the process.

Maturity Ladder With a maturity ladder, funds are invested in money market securities or deposits with consecutive rollover or maturity dates.

Suppose a corporate investor has a small amount of cash that management wants to invest. No liquidity is expected to be required for at least one month, and the maximum investment term based on the cash forecast is three months. The company uses a laddering strategy. The funds available are divided into three approximately equal amounts. A third is invested in a one-month deposit, another third in two-month deposit, and the remainder in a three-month deposit.

As each maturity occurs, the deposit is rolled over into a three-month maturity. The result is that every month a maturing deposit is available for liquidity purposes. In addition, the organization takes advantage of the slightly higher interest rates that are typically available for three-month deposits as compared with one-month deposits.

Of course, the strategy might not be appropriate if management believed that interest rates were likely to move higher in the near term. In addition, such a strategy presumes an upward-sloping yield curve, in which higher yields are available for longer maturities. This is not always the case.

Matching   Matching maturity dates to specific cash flow requirement dates is a passive technique for short-term investing. Where funds are designated for a specific purpose, passive techniques such as matching are an alternative. Rather than forecast future interest rates, investing decisions are made based on the most appropriate maturity date, within predefined limits and parameters. The maturity date for new securities is chosen, when possible, for its match with the expected requirement date for funds.

The advantage of matching is that it is relatively easy to implement and does not require active forecasting of interest rates or the yield curve. The corollary is that the performance of the portfolio will reflect the average maturity of the instruments in it, which are dictated by the organization's requirements for cash. In addition, if there is a great deal of forecast uncertainty, investments will necessarily be of shorter maturity than they otherwise would be to take the uncertainty into account. In a normal, upward-sloping yield curve environment, this means that yield will be lower for shorter maturity dates.

Outsourcing

The outsourcing of money market investment management is an alternative for organizations without the interest or internal resources to manage short-term funds in-house. Types of outsourcing include investing funds with professional money managers or in money market mutual funds, for example.

Although outsourcing often is considered to be a passive strategy, its style as passive or active more properly depends on how the funds are managed.

In many cases, cost savings can be achieved through outsourcing. For example, some not-for-profit organizations obtain very attractive pricing on pooled or mutual funds that create a compelling argument for outsourcing. Many funds offer institutional pricing for large dollar amounts with significantly lower fees.

Active Techniques

There are two major categories of active techniques for money market investment management. The first includes strategies that involve anticipating changes in interest rates or the yield curve.

The second method for active investment management focuses on altering credit quality, or alternatively anticipating a change in credit quality. Although in theory this method of investment management could be augmented by more complex techniques, such as the use of credit derivatives, in practice that is not the case. Active management can also be facilitated with the use of interest rate derivatives, such as forward rate agreements, futures, or options, which are discussed in more detail in Chapter 5.

The intent of an active investment management strategy is to earn returns that are greater than those otherwise available with more passive strategies. However, if market changes in interest rates, the yield curve, or credit quality, for example, are incorrectly anticipated, lower returns or a loss may result. If derivatives are employed, there is also a potential for trading leverage to be employed, which would compound the size of losses, as well as introducing the counterparty risks associated with derivatives.

Yield Curve Strategies   Active yield curve strategies anticipate the future structure of the yield curve to earn additional return. Riding the yield curve is one such strategy. It involves buying securities with a longer maturity than the required time horizon, with the intent of selling the securities at the required time horizon.

In an upward-sloping yield curve environment, as a money market instrument approaches maturity, yields on similar instruments decline and prices rise. By selling the instrument prior to maturity, some of this behavior can be exploited. Depending on the behavior of interest rates and the yield curve during the life of the security, this may add additional return.

Other yield curve strategies take a more specific approach based on the anticipated changes. In addition, some strategies involve interest rate derivatives, which are discussed in more detail in Chapter 5.

With active strategies, one major risk is that the interest rate forecast does not materialize, and the organization earns a lower return than otherwise expected. In addition, as with any strategy, credit risk (and counterparty risk if derivatives are used) should be monitored, since the advantages of a correct call on interest rates or the yield curve can be erased quickly if the issuer's credit rating is downgraded.

Credit Strategies   In general, an increase in risk should be accompanied by a commensurate increase in return. Credit strategies are active strategies that attempt to take advantage of the changes in assessed credit quality. For example, if a money market portfolio manager believes that a debt issuer is about to be upgraded, it may be advantageous to buy debt securities from the issuer in anticipation of the upgrade. Prior to an upgrade, prices will be lower as risk, and therefore yield, is considered to be higher.

Other credit-related investment strategies involve a reduction in credit quality of holdings in the portfolio in order to increase yield. In some large organizations, it may be possible to borrow by issuing debt at a better rate than that available from investments. The organization can issue its own debt and use the proceeds to invest in slightly lower-quality securities. The spread becomes gross income, from which adjustments for expenses and risk must be taken.

There are risks involved with credit-related strategies, including the risk of an incorrect assessment and suffering a credit loss as a result. A credit loss can range from the default of the issuer, which is very serious, to a deterioration in credit quality, which results in capital loss.

For credit strategies to be successful, a manager must be able to correctly assess credit quality independently of the assessments widely available, such as those provided by credit rating agencies. The assessment of credit risk is very complex. However, opportunities for credit strategies may arise from an issuer that is well known to the investor, such as a prime supplier or related company.

It is important to consider that credit quality can deteriorate relatively quickly, particularly if there is a concurrent liquidity, economic, or financial event. In addition, the assessments provided by credit rating agencies or independent assessment, although very useful, are not infallible. Therefore, an organization pursuing credit strategies must be comfortable with the additional risks that such strategies involve.

Management Issues

The objectives of the money market portfolio, as well as the organization's resources and risk tolerance, will help to determine the most appropriate management strategies. If an active money market investment strategy is planned, it is important to ensure that staff members have the time, market data, and knowledge they need to effectively implement such a strategy.

The objectives of the management of the money market portfolio should be detailed in the investment policy. Policy is discussed in more detail in Chapter 10. Other important considerations include availability of credit lines, dealer relationships, and portfolio management analytics.

Active portfolio management strategies typically require greater information and analytics to price individual securities, test strategies and scenarios, monitor credit developments, review changes to the portfolio, and measure and report risk and performance. This information requires analytical systems as well as appropriate control processes, both of which can add costs to the management of the portfolio.

If treasury staff members are required to manage additional functions, areas of responsibility may suffer from increased demands or additional personnel may be required. Active management requires additional time on the part of management, who must be cognizant of the risks and develop an appropriate risk management and oversight strategy that is consistent with the organization's governance.

If several currencies have material cash flows, it may be necessary to manage portfolios in more than the domestic or operating currency. Doing this may require additional dealer relationships and analytics.

The expected time availability for the funds may make it easier to defend a passive strategy where the security's maturity matches the requirement for funds.

Benchmarking Benchmarking money market portfolio returns involves comparing risk and returns to an external reference or benchmark rate to assess the portfolio's performance. Performance measurement is the completion of the investment cycle that includes developing policy, implementation, and performance reporting.

Many money market portfolios are benchmarked against published money market indices. Composite indices can also be created based on portfolio target asset allocation, such as commercial paper or T-bills. Libor (London Interbank Offered Rate) is also used as a benchmark rate. The benchmark should be representative of the portfolio holdings.

Investment Policy

Money market investing is intended to maximize returns on short-term assets and protect them from market risk and credit risk. The key attributes are risk, return, and liquidity. These three attributes work together. For example, it is usually necessary to increase risk or sacrifice liquidity to increase return. In general, short-term portfolios are more risk averse than longer-term portfolios because they have less time to recover from financial market ups and downs.

The investment policy provides specific direction on the methods that should be taken by an organization in its achievement of these attributes in its money market investment activities. In doing so, it provides a clear statement of portfolio objectives and constraints. The policy also provides treasury staff and management with a mandate, which avoids judgment of investment decisions by hindsight.

Although there are many variations, a money market investment policy typically covers these areas at a minimum:

Objectives of the Portfolio

- *Risk.* Appropriate for the portfolio and the objectives—most commonly a low-level risk for short-term liquidity portfolios
- *Liquidity.* Appropriate for the portfolio and the objectives—commonly a high level of liquidity is sought
- *Return.* Appropriate for the portfolio and the objectives—normally secondary to risk and liquidity

Standards of Care Applicable to the Portfolio's Management

- Prudence in the management of the portfolio, including the use of judgment and care
- Potential conflicts of interest and ethical considerations
- Authority and its delegation

Requirements for Financial Institutions, Safekeeping/Custodial Service Providers, and Issuers

- Internal control issues to protect funds from errors or fraud, and appropriate checks and balances to prevent unauthorized or fraudulent transactions
- Authorization of financial institutions, dealers, or custodians, including information and authorities required
- Minimum credit quality of counterparties, issuers, and custodians

Permitted Types of Investment Securities

- Government securities (e.g., Treasury bills)
- Commercial paper, if appropriate
- Certificates of deposit, if appropriate
- Other securities that are appropriate given the organization's objectives and constraints

Constraints on the Portfolio and Individual Securities

- Maximum dollar or percentage limit invested in debt and liabilities of individual issuers
- Maximum dollar or percentage limit invested by type of securities
- Maximum term to maturity for individual investments
- Requirements for diversification
- Permitted use of derivatives, if any, and restrictions
- Required action if credit quality declines
- Maximum dollar amount maturing on a given day

Reporting and Review Processes for the Portfolio

- Methodology for calculating and reporting performance
- Benchmarks for portfolio asset classes
- Frequency of repricing at current market prices (marking-to-market)
- Frequency and process for policy review and update
- Requirements for controls and audit
- Any other constraints or requirements

Managing Cash Shortfalls

Temporary cash shortfalls are a normal part of operations for many organizations. If there is a cash shortfall or negative balance, it may be necessary to arrange funding, such as a drawdown on the organization's operating line of credit, prime loan, arrangement of short-term borrowing with a lender, or the issuance of short-term debt such as bankers' acceptances or commercial paper. Strategies to fund cash shortfalls typically meet these attributes:

- Short term in nature and can be repaid easily or rolled over, as necessary, for flexibility

- Cheap to issue without significant regulatory hurdles or costs

- Quick and easy to issue and ideally can be issued in the course of a telephone call or two

Once the initial setup has been undertaken, the issuance of debt, such as commercial paper or bankers' acceptances or a drawdown on the organization's line of credit, can be facilitated. In most cases, agreements are in place in advance of the requirement for funding.

Debt Issuance

Debt securities, such as commercial paper or bankers' acceptances, can be issued to meet a demand for short-term funding. Both of these are discussed earlier in this chapter.

Where short-term securities are issued regularly, there may be loyal investor demand for securities. In this case, it may be worthwhile to issue securities regularly to maintain the favorable investor community and market for the debt. As a result, debt issuance may occur even when there is not an anticipated cash shortfall. If borrowing can be done at a lower rate than that available on appropriate risk securities, excess funds can be reinvested.

Receivables Financing

Accounts receivables financing is an alternative for financing short-term cash requirements. Also known as factoring, receivables financing may be with or without recourse. With recourse financing, which is lower cost, the lender collects from the receivables customer. The borrower is liable to the lender if the customer defaults.

With nonrecourse financing, which is more expensive, the lender collects from the receivables customer. If the customer defaults, the lender suffers the loss. A similar type of asset financing is based on company inventory.

Securitization

Securitization often is used for financing in specialized areas. Securitization involves bundling and packaging a pool of assets (e.g., customer loans) and issuing securities backed by the assets.

Credit enhancement is used to make the securities more attractive and therefore more salable to various types of investors. Complexities, including credit enhancement and legal fees, can add significant costs to these structures, which may result in them being less appropriate for short-term temporary funding.

Lines of Credit

Lines of credit provide short-term funding up to a maximum amount and term. Offered by financial institutions, they are commonly used for financing short-term cash requirements. Lines of credit provide borrowers with access to funds up to a maximum (the credit limit) for a period of time, and they are popular due to their ease of use and simplicity.

Lines may be secured with collateral, such as accounts receivable, or unsecured and granted on the general credit quality of the borrower. Revolving lines of credit can be drawn down and repaid as frequently as desired, to the maximum credit limit.

Borrowers should be aware that lines of credit may require payment of a commitment fee to keep the line available, which may be required whether the line is used or not. In addition, restrictions may prevent a line of credit from having an outstanding balance maintained throughout the year. As a result, for organizations that use their line of credit regularly, it may be necessary to pay it down in its entirety at least once per year for a minimum specific term (a cleanup period) according to the terms of the agreement. Doing this helps to assure the lender that the line of credit is not being used for long-term financing.

In addition, if funding is based on the availability of a line of credit, changes at the lending financial institution may cause the line of credit to not be renewed. In this case, the organization may have to find alternative sources of credit.

Summary

- The money market is the market for cash and short-term liabilities and debt securities.

- Money market investment assets can be managed using active or passive strategies. The decision will depend on several factors, including the organization's approach to cash management.

- Alternatives are available for meeting short-term cash funding requirements, including receivables financing, securitization, and lines of credit.

Note

1. See the Securities and Exchange Commission web site for more information on SEC rules (*www.sec.gov*).

CHAPTER 4

Foreign Exchange Management

After reading this chapter, you should be able to:

- Differentiate methods for reducing foreign exchange exposure.
- Evaluate foreign exchange instruments for managing foreign exchange risk.
- Appreciate the attributes of foreign exchange derivatives.

Foreign Exchange Market

Foreign exchange requirements arise from the commercial transactions of an organization, including purchases from suppliers and vendors and sales to customers in other countries and currencies.

Foreign exchange requirements also arise as a result of foreign currency assets or liabilities. In addition, foreign exchange requirements may be influenced by exposure to commodities prices, if prices are denominated in a currency other than the domestic currency, and by the location and activities of major competitors. This is discussed in more detail in Chapter 6.

Most foreign exchange trading occurs between large organizations, especially between large international financial institutions. The largest foreign exchange trading centers, as measured by trading volume, are London and New York. Together, these two geographic centers account for about half of all trading.

The major participants in foreign exchange trading are large banks and financial institutions, which together account for a large majority of trading. Corporations and governments also conduct major volumes as they manage global commercial and financing activities.

Foreign Exchange Exposure

Exposure Reduction

Most organizations are affected directly or indirectly by foreign exchange exposure. The nature of foreign exchange exposure is that even purely domestic businesses may have exposure. For example, currency exposure may arise when the currency of international competitors weakens or as a result of commodity-related purchases or sales.

Because foreign exchange exposure arises from many of the commercial and financial transactions of an organization, it is sometimes possible to reduce exposure and therefore risk. Several techniques

IN THE REAL WORLD

Foreign Exchange Trading

Global foreign exchange trading volumes are about $1.9 trillion per day, based on a triennial survey conducted in 2004 by central banks and the Bank for International Settlements.[a] The most widely traded currency is the U.S. dollar. In addition, euro, Japanese yen, and British sterling also have major trading volumes.

[a] Bank for International Settlements, Monetary and Economic Department, Triennial Central Bank Survey of Foreign Exchange and Derivatives Market Activity in April 2004.

TIPS & TECHNIQUES

The Euro

The introduction of the euro currency in 1999 established an unprecedented level of economic and currency cooperation between a number of European countries. The euro replaced the legacy currencies of these countries (as of May 2005):

Austria	Germany	Luxembourg
Belgium	Greece	Netherlands
Finland	Ireland	Portugal
France	Italy	Spain

Several other small European countries or jurisdictions, such as Monaco, also use the euro.

attempt to take advantage of natural opportunities for hedging through changes in business activities. These include:

- Netting currencies between related companies or operations

- Foreign currency debt

- Changes to purchasing and/or processing

- Transfer exchange rate risk

- Hedging exposure to some currencies with other currencies

It is important to note that exposure reduction strategies may be impacted by local legal, tax, or reporting issues. Therefore, these strategies need to be considered carefully prior to implementation.

Currency Netting

Currency netting involves aggregating foreign exchange payments and receipts that are made between parts of an organization, and sometimes with outside organizations, to reduce the necessity for external purchase and sale activities. By centralizing some of its banking activities in-house, currency from parts of the organization with excess currency can be made available to parts of the organization that require it. Intercompany transactions can be booked at market exchange rates or may include a small price spread if appropriate.

When an organization has foreign currency cash inflows and outflows, a cash forecast for each currency assists in identifying currency exposures. The forecast format should enable the user to determine an expected balance for each currency, as well as whether there is expected to be a cumulative deficit or excess currency over time with reasonable certainty. Cumulative gaps between cash inflows and outflows are useful to track because they may require hedging, in contrast to cash flows that offset over time and that effectively represent a timing issue. Foreign currency cash forecasts are discussed in more detail in Chapter 2.

Foreign Currency Debt

There are several reasons for borrowing in a foreign currency. Issuers may want to entice specific institutional investors by issuing in a desirable currency. Lower foreign interest rates might be seen as a way to reduce funding costs. Foreign currency debt may be required to finance an overseas expansion or investment in foreign plant and operations. Sometimes the issuance of foreign currency debt can reduce foreign exchange exposure.

When there is a mismatch between foreign currency assets and liabilities, there is potential for loss. The risk of debt denominated in a foreign currency may be reduced if the borrower has offsetting assets denominated in the same currency, such as an income-producing subsidiary, for example. If foreign currency income is adequate to offset payments on the liability, and it can be expected to continue for the life of the debt, the organization may be able to use it as a natural hedge for exposure purposes. Doing this may provide lower foreign currency borrowing rates while reducing the exchange rate risk already inherent in foreign currency receivables. If the foreign currency strengthens and the market value of the debt increases, the value of the offsetting foreign currency revenues should also increase.

However, when foreign currency debt is offset with foreign currency revenues, it does not take into account how customer demand and revenues might change in response to exchange rates. Foreign

IN THE REAL WORLD

Foreign Currency Debt

The market value of unhedged foreign currency debt will fluctuate as exchange rates change. Foreign currency debt is sometimes issued in an environment of low foreign currency interest rates. However, the value of the outstanding debt can increase significantly if exchange rates move adversely and there is no hedge to offset the changes.

The effect of exchange rate changes on foreign currency debt can be seen in this table, which shows the translated value of a CAD$20 million liability to a U.S. borrower under four exchange rate scenarios ranging from CAD$1.4300/USD to CAD$1.1300 /USD.

Exchange Rate (CAD/USD)	Translated Liability in U.S. Dollars
CAD$1.4300 /USD	US$13,986,013
CAD$1.3300 /USD	US$15,037,593
CAD$1.2300 /USD	US$16,260,162
CAD$1.1300 /USD	US$17,699,115

currency revenues may be sensitive to exchange rates, particularly major changes. Changes in exchange rates that impact revenues may affect the organization's ability to service debt denominated in foreign currency.

Changes to Internal Operations

Foreign exchange exposure can sometimes be reduced through changes to suppliers, sources of materials, or locations for manufacturing. For example a company with foreign currency sales might use a supplier that prices its products in the same currency as the company's sales. Realistically, there should be reasons other than currency for making changes to supplier or operational relationships, because disrupting long-term relationships is a major initiative.

Longer-term strategies might involve manufacturing in key customer locations or obtaining new customers where inputs are sourced. Exploiting exchange rate differences is often a reason to relocate manufacturing or sourcing, although there are usually other reasons.

Transfer Exchange Rate Risk

Transferring exchange rate risk to customers or suppliers is a strategy for minimizing exchange rate risk. For example, pricing surcharges help to offset exchange rate risk and pass the risk on to the customer. In some industries, when exchange rates change dramatically, a currency surcharge is added to the final price.

When it is possible to obtain fixed prices in two currencies from suppliers, one way to minimize currency risk is to pay the lower of the two prices when the invoice is paid. This is an advantage to the customer but a disadvantage to the seller, which has uncertainty over its own exchange rate risk.

Other strategies include invoicing foreign customers in their own or a major currency. If an organization already has foreign exchange exposure through purchases, this may help to offset some of its other exposure. When pricing changes are made, they should be permanent changes to currencies that are widely traded, such as U.S. dollars or euros. Prices should be offered in one currency, not a choice of currencies, since the latter increases uncertainty and therefore risk.

TIPS & TECHNIQUES

Project Bids

Bids on foreign projects often require a foreign exchange rate component to be embedded in the price of the contract. There is a risk that rates may change dramatically once the bid has been submitted but before notification to the winning bidder occurs. Some companies manage this risk by inserting a currency adjustment clause into the contract. If the exchange rate moves more than a predetermined amount, the contract price must be adjusted to reflect the exchange rate change. This clause shifts exchange rate risk to the purchaser. Compound options, discussed later in this chapter, are also used for bid situations.

Negotiating fixed price contracts with suppliers also shifts foreign exchange risk to a supplier. However, if the supplier does a poor job of managing the risk, product prices may be expected to rise to offset exchange rate losses. In many instances, prices that rise are slow to subsequently fall. In addition, fixed price contracts may have limits or other restrictions. As a result, fixed price supplier contracts provide a lag time before exchange rate changes affect pricing.

Proxy Hedging

An organization may find that it is difficult to obtain fair pricing for currencies that are not actively traded. The exchange rate may be controlled or hedging products unavailable. In addition, an organization may have exposure to several correlated regional currencies, with the amounts of each too small for an effective hedging program.

Currencies, such as those within regional areas, sometimes exhibit a high correlation to one another. This correlation may be due to similar economic or political prospects or highly regional trade, for example in emerging market currencies. If there is strong correlation between the currencies, one currency might be used for hedging purposes in place of others.

In general, hedging one currency with another introduces the risk that the currency being hedged will continue to be highly correlated with the proxy currency. Past correlations may not be indicative of future correlations, and they do not provide a forecast of future exchange rates. Political or economic instability can dramatically affect a country's exchange rate in isolation from any regional factors. As a result, a proxy hedge could result in an organization being unhedged or under- or overhedged. Obviously, the trade-off between protection and risk must be weighed carefully and the exposure managed accordingly.

Foreign Exchange Basics

Foreign exchange rates are the relative prices of currencies, as determined by market supply and demand. Exchange rates fluctuate almost constantly.

Foreign Exchange Price Quotes

An exchange rate expresses the relative value of two currencies, and as a result, an exchange rate can be quoted in terms of either currency.

The quoted currency is the currency that fluctuates in amount as the exchange rate fluctuates. The currency that does not fluctuate in amount when the exchange rate fluctuates and that represents one unit of a currency is known as the *base currency*. The U.S. dollar is most often the base currency in interbank trading, and exchange rates quoted with the U.S. dollar as base currency are said to be quoted in the indirect method. For example, 115.00 Japanese yen per US dollar is an indirect quote, while 0.008696 U.S. dollars per yen is a direct quote.

Currencies such as euro, British sterling, Australian dollar, and New Zealand dollar commonly function as the base currency when they trade in the interbank market. Exchange rates with one of these currencies as the base currency are said be quoted in the direct method. For example, 1.2500 U.S. dollars per euro is a direct quote.

Most exchange rates are quoted to four decimal places when they trade in the interbank market. One notable exception is Japanese yen, which is quoted as Japanese yen per U.S. dollar to two decimal places. Some pricing examples are:

2.2100–2.2110	Canadian dollars per British sterling
1.2190–1.2200	Canadian dollars per U.S. dollar
0.8197–0.8203	U.S. dollars per Canadian dollar
115.20–115.25	Japanese yen per U.S. dollar

An exchange rate can be expressed as a function of either currency. The base currency can be changed by calculating the exchange rate's inverse, although rounding naturally introduces inaccuracies.

Calculating the reciprocal of the exchange rate converts an indirect quote to a direct quote, or vice versa. When calculating reciprocal rates, rounding conventions exist. When the inverse of an interbank exchange rate is calculated, convention is that the number of decimal places should be three greater than the places before the decimal. For example, Japanese yen is quoted as 115.00 per U.S. dollar in the interbank

TIPS & TECHNIQUES

Orders

Foreign exchange markets trade 24 hours a day. Many organizations choose levels at which they would like to buy or sell a currency and leave orders with their financial institution. An order is an agreement to buy or sell a specified amount of currency at the order price should it be reached. Orders are often placed in overnight markets or during local holidays to take advantage of market fluctuations in overseas markets outside local business hours.

market. To calculate the reciprocal, there are three places in front of the decimal, so the inverted price quote should be rounded to 6 (3 + 3) decimal places, or 0.008696 U.S. dollars per yen. Particular care should be taken to determine which method of quoting is used when currencies have nearly equal values and may fluctuate above or below par.

A point is an increment or decrement in the last standard decimal place of an exchange rate. For most currencies, a point is an increase or decrease of one at the fourth decimal place. One notable exception is Japanese yen, which is normally quoted to two decimal places in interbank trading (and six decimal places in the inverse). Points are sometimes divided into smaller units when interest rate differentials between two currencies are very narrow or the price is very competitive. For example, the one-month forward price for a currency may be shown as 5.5 points.

An exchange rate between two currencies, in which neither is the U.S. dollar, is known as a cross rate. There are active cross-rate markets in several major currencies, such as British sterling, euro, and Japanese yen.

Bid-Offer

A basic trading protocol exists in foreign exchange markets as in other markets. When two-sided (bid and offer) prices are given, the dealer making the price has the right to the favorable rate. In the foreign exchange market, this means buying the base currency at the lower rate and selling the base currency at the higher rate. This protocol exists when banks and dealers trade with one another, as well as when they trade with customers. The dealer, in making prices to others, has the right to deal at its own preferred prices when transacting with another dealer who is calling for a price.

Foreign Exchange Settlement

The foreign exchange settlement date, also known as the value date or delivery date, is the day that funds are exchanged between counterparties to a foreign exchange transaction.

In general, the term "spot settlement" means a transaction for (more or less) immediate delivery. In the foreign exchange markets, the term spot refers to settlement two business days after the transaction is booked (T+2). For specific exceptions, such as spot transactions involving North American currencies, spot is the next business day (T+1). This time lag provides time for funds to be transferred regardless of time zones.

Currencies usually settle electronically as debits or credits in correspondent financial institutions in other time zones. As a result, by convention, spot transactions are normally settled one or two business days after the trade date. This provides time for both parties to make good settlement, since money center banks must be open in order to make or receive foreign currency payments.

A bank in New York transacting currency business on behalf of its customers can easily settle U.S. dollars by making or accepting U.S. dollar payments. However, it will use other international banks internationally to settle its Japanese yen, euro, and other foreign currency transactions. These foreign banks, operating on behalf of the New York bank, are its international correspondent banks.

A significant proportion of foreign exchange volume is interbank trading. Given the settlement delays caused by various global time zones, foreign exchange trading creates settlement risk. A major initiative to reduce the risk arising from nonsimultaneous foreign exchange settlements is Continuous Linked Settlement (CLS). CLS began operations in 2002 and is supported by dozens of the world's largest banks. It is discussed in more detail in Chapter 8.

Transactions for same-day settlement are known as cash transactions, not to be confused with transactions involving physical banknotes. The cash exchange rate reflects the money market interest rate differential between spot and the cash date for the two currencies. Same-day transactions are not possible for overseas currencies, as a result of time differences, because local banks in the overseas centers will have already ceased operations for the day. As a result, it is not possible at 11 a.m. in New York to transact cash euros. However, cash transactions are common between regional currencies, such as U.S. and Canadian dollars that are both within North American time zones, but they must be transacted early in the day.

Foreign Exchange Forwards

A foreign exchange forward is a bilateral agreement to purchase or sell a predetermined amount of currency for a future delivery date. Most

FX Forward Dates

Standard forward contract terms are one month, two month, three month, six month, and one year. The maturity of a forward is calculated from the spot date. Therefore, a one-month forward when spot is June 15 will mature on July 15. If July 15 is not a business day (for either currency), the forward date will be the next business day for both currencies. The exception occurs when spot is the last business day of the month and the forward is for a standard term of one month or greater. In that case, the forward date automatically shifts to the last business day of the forward month, regardless of the number of days. For example, if today is January 30 and spot is January 31 (the last business day of January), the one-month forward date will be February 28 (the last business day of February), regardless of the number of days. If February 28 is not a business day for both currencies, the date will move back to the last "good" date (e.g., February 27).

These trading conventions for standard forward dates mean that a one-month forward contract might have from 28 to 33 days. As a result, a forward price may change even when interest rate differentials do not, simply due to the change in the number of days.

A forward contract may be booked for any customized date. Currency forward prices for nonstandard forward dates are extrapolated from actively traded standard forwards. Standard forwards are most often used by traders for position taking and hedging. However, all forward prices are constantly evaluated by traders against money market rates for pricing discrepancies that present arbitrage opportunities. These activities provide liquidity to the marketplace.

forward contracts have a specific delivery date, although other varieties, including nondeliverable forwards and flexible forwards, also exist.

Most forwards mature within one to two years, although there is no theoretical maximum maturity date. Forwards trade actively between dealers and with customers, and the forward price generally includes a profit for the dealer. The forward market for major currencies is liquid, due in part to the fact that forwards can be replicated using money market instruments.

A forward price consists of a spot price plus or minus forward points that represent the interest rate differential between the two currencies. Whether these points are added to or subtracted from the spot price depends on whether the forward rate is at a discount or premium. This in turn depends on whether the domestic interest rate is higher or lower than the foreign interest rate. For example, if Canadian dollar interest rates are higher than U.S. interest rates, the forward points are added to the spot rate (quoted in the indirect method) making the Canadian dollar cheaper in the forward market. The forward price makes the purchaser of the higher yielding Canadian dollar indifferent between taking delivery now or at the forward date. Together, the forward points and the spot rate are known as the all-in forward rate.

Forward Prices

Forward points may increase or decrease the spot rate. Normally, rates are quoted on data services without positive or negative signs. If the bid is greater than the offer (e.g., 60 − 55), the forward points reduce the forward rate as compared with the spot rate (i.e., they are subtracted from the spot rate), and the exchange rate is said to be at a discount in the forward market. If the bid is lower than the offer (e.g., 60 − 65), the

IN THE REAL WORLD

Forward Rates

Here is an example of forward prices (Japanese yen per U.S. dollar) for several standard forward dates.

Maturity	Forward Points	All-in Forward Rate
Spot		104.95 JPY/USD
1 month	−20	104.75
2 months	−35	104.60
3 months	−50	104.45
6 months	−90	104.05
1 year	−160	103.35
2 year	−240	102.55

forward points increase the forward rate as compared with the spot rate. The exchange rate is said to be at a premium in the forward market.

The forward exchange rate represents the interest rate differential between two currencies. If it did not, arbitrage could achieve a risk-free profit for traders. Traders arbitrage by replicating the components of a forward using the interest rate markets, by borrowing and investing, and vice versa. The opportunity to arbitrage ensures liquidity in the foreign exchange forward markets.

Nondeliverable Forwards

Nondeliverable forwards are contractual agreements where an exchange of the currency does not occur. Similar to a cash-settled futures contract, at the forward date, the current spot rate is compared to the

TIPS & TECHNIQUES

Flexible Forwards

A variation on a standard forward contract is an option-dated or flexible forward. These forward contracts permit the forward to be used, within a predetermined date range, when it is most convenient. Some contracts permit the forward to be utilized in up to three separate deliveries, providing additional flexibility.

Flexible forwards can be useful for organizations that find it difficult to forecast a specific exchange date. The price will not change if the forward is used at the first possible date or the last possible date. Due to the fact that a financial institution cannot forecast when, within the permitted date range, a flexible forward will be used, flexible forwards are usually priced either to the start date or end date, whichever is least favorable from the customer's standpoint. As a result, their flexibility involves a cost.

contracted forward rate and a cash payment changes hands. No settlement of the foreign currency occurs. Nondeliverable forwards often are used for hedging emerging market currencies.

Currency Futures

Currency futures are standardized forward contracts that trade on an organized exchange. Contract sizes, expiry dates, and trading and settlement rules are standardized by the exchange on which they trade.

Many exchanges offer currency futures, including:

- International Monetary Market (IMM) division of the Chicago Mercantile Exchange

- New York Board of Trade

- Philadelphia Stock Exchange

Unlike forward contracts, there is no requirement for a line of credit with a financial institution to transact a futures contract. Futures contracts are transacted through a broker or futures commission merchant. Futures contracts are contractual obligations and both margin (see "In the Real World: Futures Margin") and transaction commissions apply to them.

U.S. exchanges quote currency futures prices in U.S. dollars per foreign currency unit. Performance of parties to a futures contract is guaranteed by a clearing corporation, replacing credit risk of any individual contract holder with exposure to the clearing corporation.

IN THE REAL WORLD

Futures Margin

Futures margin is a small deposit used to control a larger position in the futures contract. It is a performance bond, deposited with the futures broker that facilitated the transaction, that helps to ensure the performance of both the futures buyer and seller. Exchanges determine minimum margin, depending on the contract size and type of position, and exchange members (brokers) may require additional margin.

Futures contracts are repriced daily, and each margin account is debited or credited with the day's losses or gains. When the market value of a futures position declines, additional margin may be required. Failure to respond to a margin call may result in the position being closed out at the expense of the account holder.

Swaps

Swaps are contractual agreements between two parties that provide for an exchange of currencies. Foreign exchange swaps tend to be shorter in term and have two exchanges between counterparties. Currency swaps tend to be longer in term and involve multiple exchanges between counterparties. Structurally, they can be very similar to one another or quite different, depending on the specifics of the contracts. Swaps trade primarily in the over-the-counter market between large financial institutions and their customers.

Foreign Exchange Swaps

A foreign exchange swap consists of a spot transaction and a forward transaction. One currency is bought at the spot date and rate, and the transaction is reversed at the forward date and rate. Both spot and forward price are set at the outset, and the difference (the forward points) is the net cost or gain resulting from the swap. Foreign exchange swaps are used extensively to manage cash balances and exposures in various currencies. Forward trading is also facilitated using swaps.

Foreign exchange swaps are often used to facilitate short-term investing or borrowing in other currencies. Although they are foreign exchange transactions, they effectively function as an investment in one currency and a loan in another. Foreign exchange swaps usually have a term of about a year or less, although there is no theoretical maximum. Chapter 3 provides an example of a foreign exchange swap used for cash management purposes.

Currency Swaps

Currency swaps enable two parties to exchange their respective payments, changing the effective nature of an asset or liability without altering the underlying exposure. Currency swaps usually have periodic payments between the counterparties for the term of the swap and cover a longer period of time than foreign exchange swaps.

A currency swap is similar to a loan combined with an investment. An exchange takes place at the beginning of the currency swap for the desired currency. Over the term of the swap, each party makes regular periodic interest payments on the currency received and receives periodic interest payments on the currency given up. Payments usually are not netted because they are in different currencies. An exchange back to the original currencies occurs at the swap's maturity, so there is no foreign exchange risk on the principal.

A currency swap sometimes involves only a change in the currency. A currency basis swap (or floating-to-floating swap) involves a change in the currency and in the floating interest rate known as the basis. Most commonly, a currency swap involves both a change in the currency and a change from floating to fixed (or vice versa).

The need for a currency swap might arise from a company's long-term foreign currency debt issue, for example. A currency swap might be used to convert the foreign currency payments to payments in the domestic currency. Currency swaps can also be used to lock in the cost of existing foreign currency debt or for changing the revenue stream on an asset.

TIPS & TECHNIQUES

Currency Swaps

Currency swaps allow companies to borrow in markets where they have inherent advantages such as:

- Well-known issuer name

- Investor demand for foreign currency debt issues

- Regulatory or tax advantages that reduce costs of issue or financing

- Local government programs or subsidies that favor certain types of debt or that make a foreign currency debt issue more attractive than a similar domestic issue

Foreign Exchange Options

Foreign exchange options are similar to insurance contracts. The option buyer purchases a contract that provides protection for a particular currency (the underlying currency) beyond a predetermined exchange rate. The option buyer receives protection against adverse exchange rates, while maintaining the flexibility to take advantage of more favorable exchange rates.

A call option permits the call option buyer to buy the underlying currency at the strike rate. A put option permits the put option buyer to sell the underlying currency at the strike rate. Currency transactions always involve the sale of one currency and the purchase of another currency. As a result, a currency option is a put option on one currency and a call option on the other currency.

In exchange for paying option premium to the option seller, the option buyer obtains the right, but not the obligation, to exercise the option if it is favorable to do so. The purchase of an option provides protection beyond the strike rate for the contracted amount while maintaining the flexibility to take advantage of favorable exchange rates. From the option buyer's standpoint, the maximum loss associated with the purchase of a currency option is the premium paid, although there may be other losses related to the option buyer's currency exposure.

The foreign exchange option contract sets out the contractual details including:

- *Strike price.* The exchange rate at which the underlying currency can be bought or sold according to the terms of the option contract

- *Notional contract amount.* The amount of currency that can be sold or bought according to the terms of the option contract

- *Expiry date.* The date at which the option contract, if not exercised, expires

- *Exercise.* How and when the option contract can be exercised (or used) by the option buyer

In exchange for receiving option premium from the option buyer, the option seller takes on the obligation to deliver or accept delivery of the underlying currency at the strike price if the option is exercised by the option buyer. The option seller has considerably more risk than the option buyer, and it is not always possible to quantify the maximum loss to the option seller. The option buyer decides whether to exercise the option or not.

An option is said to be in-the-money if it has intrinsic value. An option that is in-the-money can be exercised at an exchange rate that is more favorable than current exchange rates. An option that is at-the-money can be exercised at an exchange rate equal to that in the market. An option that is out-of-the-money can be exercised at an exchange rate that is worse than currently available in the market, but its value arises from the possibility that it may be worth exercising in the future.

At expiry, if the option is in-the-money, the option holder can exercise it or sell it. If neither is undertaken in a timely manner, it is theoretically possible for an in-the-money option to inadvertently be permitted to expire. The decision to exercise an option is at the discretion of the option buyer, and the decision must be communicated in a timely manner according to the terms of the contract.

Option holders with in-the-money options that want to exercise their options must ensure they inform the financial institution or broker prior to the notice deadline. If the notice deadline is not met, the option may expire unexercised and worthless, although some contracts have provisions for automatic exercise of in-the-money options. Some exchange-traded options offer automatic exercise if certain conditions are met.

Options that have value but are no longer required can be sold prior to expiry. If an option is not in-the-money by the time it expires, it will expire worthless. European-style options are exercisable only on the expiry date, while American-style options are exercisable any time until and including the expiry date, although other exercise variations exist.

Options are traded in the over-the-counter market or on organized exchanges. In North America, currency options trade at the Philadelphia Stock Exchange and the Chicago Mercantile Exchange.

IN THE REAL WORLD

Intrinsic Value and Time Value

Option premiums consist of intrinsic value and time value. Together, time value and intrinsic value comprise the option's value. Intrinsic value is the amount an option is in-the-money, if any. Intrinsic value is positive or zero. Time value is the market's estimate of the probability of an option becoming in-the-money prior to expiry if it is not already. Time value is positive or zero.

Option pricing depends on several factors, including the volatility of the exchange rate and the time remaining to the option's expiry. The more volatile the currency, the greater the chance for it to be exercised and the more premium the option seller will demand for the option, all else being equal. These factors influence the option's time value.

An option's time value does not change in a linear fashion with the passage of time. Time value erodes much more rapidly as the option approaches expiry. As the option approaches expiry, presuming it is not yet in-the-money, the chances of it being exercisable before expiry become very small.

The sale of an option has a considerably different risk profile from the purchase of an option. The option seller receives option premium and is obligated to the terms of the option. As a result, the maximum loss or worst-case scenario associated with an option may not be determinable in advance.

Organizations that sell options must be comfortable with the risks associated with such a strategy. The sale of an option does not provide a hedge against outstanding exposure, although the premium received provides some cushion against adverse exchange rates. The risk of an adverse currency fluctuation must be managed proactively, and the option seller may have to take additional measures if the currency moves adversely.

Foreign Exchange Collar

A collar is an option-based strategy that combines the purchase of an option and the sale of an option, both with the same expiry date and on the same currencies. Foreign exchange collars often are used to reduce the cost of hedging using options. A collar strategy sometimes is known as a range forward, cylinder option, tunnel option, or zero-cost option. When combined, the two options provide an exchange rate range for the user. Although there are many other option strategies, collars commonly are used for managing foreign exchange risk.

The upper and lower bands of the collar are created by the strike rate of the purchased and sold options. To provide protection against an increase in an exchange rate, the purchase of a call is combined with the sale of a put. The call's strike price becomes the upper band, while the put's strike price creates the lower band.

If rates move outside the collar, either the call or the put will be exercised. However, if the exchange rate remains below the call strike rate and above the put strike rate, neither option will be exercised. Collars effectively limit the user's exchange rate to the upper and lower strike prices for the notional amount of the contract.

The strike prices of the purchased and sold options are often adjusted so that the premium from the option that is sold is partially or fully offset by the premium paid for the purchased option. The collar provides protection at a specified rate (strike rate of the purchased option) while giving up benefits of favorable rate movements beyond a certain point (strike rate of the sold option). A collar with net option premiums of zero is often referred to as a "zero-cost" collar. The component options are usually European-style, so that one or the other is exercised at expiry but not both.

Average Rate Options

An average rate, or Asian, option is a customized foreign exchange option. The payoff of an average rate option depends on the difference between the average exchange rate over the option's term and the strike rate. Another less common variation has a floating strike rate that is compared to the exchange rate at the option's expiry date.

Average rate options are often used where foreign exchange transactions occur on an ongoing and regular basis, such as the receipt of foreign currency payments every month. Depending on the type of average rate option used and the contract's specifics, they may provide a less expensive hedge than other types of options.

Barrier Options

A barrier option is typically a European-style option that becomes exercisable ("knock-in") or unexercisable ("knock-out") when the exchange rate passes a predetermined barrier level specified in the contract. The payoff of a barrier option is contingent on the exchange rate reaching the barrier level. Once reached, the option may become exercisable in the case of a knock-in option or become unexercisable in the case of a knock-out option.

Knock-in options may be of the *up-and-in* or *down-and-in* variety, while knock-out options may be of the *up-and-out* or *down-and-out* variety, depending on the terms of the contract.

Barrier levels need to be chosen carefully. Because of the possibility of an option being knocked out, the barrier exchange rate may be chosen as a level at which an option is no longer required. For knock-in options, the barrier rate might be an exchange rate at which an option is desirable. Knocked-out options that have to be replaced to maintain protection will increase the overall cost of hedging.

Compound Options

Compound options are options on options. They provide the compound option buyer with the right, but not the obligation, to enter into an option contract at the compound option's expiry date for a predetermined option premium. Although they usually are cheaper to purchase initially than standard options, if the compound option is exercised and the underlying put or call purchased, the total cost may be greater than that associated with an ordinary put or call option.

Compound options have been used to protect against currency exposure during the bidding process in international projects denominated in foreign currencies. There may be a significant time lag between project tender pricing and the announcement of the successful winner. In exchange for option premium, an organization can hedge the cost of an option that may be required if the contract is won. Contracts are normally European-style options that can be exercised at maturity.

Group of 31 Report

The Group of 31: Core Principles for Managing Multinational FX Risk report arose from a 1998 study of foreign exchange risk management

TIPS & TECHNIQUES

FX Credit Facility

Foreign exchange (FX) transactions with a financial institution require credit facilities. The process is similar to that involved with obtaining other credit. Credit facilities are usually required for any foreign exchange or derivatives transactions.

Typically, the use of the line is based on a percentage of the notional amount of contracts transacted. For example, suppose a $10 million foreign exchange forward contract requires a credit allocation of 10 to 15 percent of the contract amount. Therefore, the forward contract would utilize $1 to $1.5 million of the available credit facility.

Although not common, a financial institution may require collateral or margin to transact a forward, particularly for long-dated forwards, where there is significant market movement in exchange rates, or where the financial institution has concerns about the counterparty's credit risk.

by multinational corporations.[1] The project was undertaken by Greenwich Treasury Advisors LLC and sponsored by General Motors.

The study surveyed 31 large multinational corporations with foreign exchange exposure arising from business activities, 13 of them American, as well as 2 Japanese and 13 European companies. Average sales were $50 billion. A follow-up study looked at the activities of an additional 33 U.S. multinational corporations with average sales of $11 billion.

Twelve core principles for managing foreign exchange exposure emerged as principles used by a majority of firms. These principles cover fundamental principles, principles related to trading volume, and principles related to risk appetite. They are:

Fundamental Principles

1. *Document Foreign Exchange Policy.* Document a foreign exchange policy approved by senior management or the Board of Directors. Critical policy elements include: hedging objectives, hedgeable exposures, hedging time horizon, authorized foreign exchange derivatives, the extent to which positions can be managed upon views of future foreign exchange rates, compensation for foreign exchange trader performance, and hedging performance measures.

2. *Hire Well-Qualified, Experienced Personnel.* Have a sufficient number of qualified, experienced personnel to properly execute the company's foreign exchange policy.

3. *Centralize Foreign Exchange Trading and Risk Management.* Centralize the foreign exchange trading and risk management with Parent Treasury, which may be assisted by foreign hedging centers reporting to Parent Treasury.

4. *Adopt Uniform Foreign Exchange Accounting Procedures.* Require uniform foreign exchange accounting procedures, uniform exchange rates for book purposes, and multicurrency general ledgers for all foreign exchange transactions. Monthly, reconcile Parent Treasury's foreign exchange hedging results to the group's consolidated generally accepted accounting principles (GAAP) foreign exchange results.

5. *Manage Foreign Exchange Forecast Error.* If anticipated foreign exchange exposures are being hedged, manage the forecast error and take steps to minimize it to the greatest extent possible.

6. *Measure Hedging Performance.* Use several performance measures to fully evaluate historic hedging effectiveness. Evaluate current hedging performance by frequently marking-to-market both the outstanding hedges and the underlying exposures.

Trading–Volume Related Principles

7. *Segregate the Back Office Function.* Segregate back office operations such as confirmations and settlements from trading. If trading volume is sufficient, use nostro accounts and net settle.

8. *Manage Counter Party Risk.* Have credit rating standards and evaluate counter party risk at least quarterly. Measure credit exposure using market valuations, not notional amounts, against assigned counter party credit limits. Use ISDA (International Swaps and Derivatives Association) or other kinds of master agreements with at least major counterparties.

9. *Buy Derivatives Competitively.* Execute the foreign exchange policy by competitively buying foreign exchange derivatives with appropriate trading controls.

Risk–Appetite Related Principles

10. *Use Pricing Models and Systems.* Have in-house pricing models for all derivatives used. Use automated systems to track, manage, and value the derivatives traded and the underlying business exposures being hedged.

11. *Measure Foreign Exchange Risk.* Understand the full nature of the foreign exchange risks being managed with a combination of risk measures such as value–at–risk, sensitivity analysis, and stress testing.

12. *Oversee Treasury's Risk Management.* Independently oversee Treasury's risk management with a Risk Committee to review and approve Treasury's risk-taking activities and strategies, exposure and counterparty credit limits, and exceptions to corporate foreign exchange policy. Depending upon the level of foreign exchange risks being managed, have either a part-time or a dedicated function to review Treasury's compliance with approved risk management policies and procedures.

Summary

- Foreign exchange exposure arises from the many commercial and financial activities of organizations.
- It may be possible to reduce foreign exchange exposure by making changes to the operational components of business.
- Foreign exchange forwards, futures, swaps, and options can be used to reduce foreign exchange risk.

Note

1. *The Group of 31 Report: Core Principles for Managing Multinational FX Risk,* Jeffrey B. Wallace, Managing Partner, Greenwich Treasury Advisors LLC. The Group of 31/Greenwich Treasury Advisors LLC. Copyright (c) 1999 by Greenwich Treasury Advisors LLC, 127 W. Putnam Avenue, Greenwich, CT 06830.

CHAPTER 5

Interest Rate Management

After reading this chapter, you should be able to:

- Understand alternatives for managing exposure to interest rates.
- Evaluate the use of forward rate agreements, futures, swaps, and options for managing interest rate risk.
- Identify key interest rate risks.

Introduction

Interest rate risks arise from the many and varied financial activities of an organization. Risks arise from commercial transactions such as extending credit, long-term borrowing to fund new projects, or as a result of portfolio holdings of fixed income securities, for example.

In general, interest rate markets are dominated by a country's domestic currency trading. However, global organizations also have global exposures that need to be managed.

Exposure Reduction

Interest rates are a key input to many financial decisions. Changes in interest rates can impact profitability. One alternative for managing interest rate risk is to organize business activities to minimize sources of interest rate exposure. Financial risks that remain then can be evaluated and managed using various financial instruments or operational techniques.

Although it is possible to reduce interest rate exposure by combining business exposures and processes, legal, tax, and regulatory ramifications may have to be taken into consideration. This is particularly true where foreign currencies or transborder transactions are involved. Some techniques that have been used to reduce interest rate exposure include:

- Global cash netting, where one part of the organization functions as an in-house cash management bank, providing intercompany lending and borrowing

- Embedded options in debt issues

- Enhanced cash flow management

- Improving asset-liability management

Intercompany Transactions

Organizations with cash flows in multiple currencies may find it beneficial to consider cash netting to reduce the need for external borrowing in key currencies. A cash forecast for specific currencies enables expected surpluses and shortfalls to be identified. On a centralized basis, it may be possible to pool funds from divisions or subsidiaries and make them available to other parts of the organization.

An intercompany netting center can also be used to reduce the number of payment transactions between related companies. In global organizations, bilateral or multilateral currency netting reduces intercompany payments and the foreign exchange transactions that the group otherwise would undertake. Netting is discussed in more detail in Chapter 10.

Intercompany lending is a longer-term approach to managing funding shortages and surpluses across an organization. The combination of companies with excess cash and a need for borrowing may reduce interest costs and permit more control over the borrowing process. As with other techniques, such as cash netting and pooling, expert assistance should be obtained to ensure that legal, tax, and regulatory restrictions or prohibitions do not exist.

Embedded Options

Embedded options associated with debt securities may provide issuers with an alternative for managing interest rate risk. Embedded options include callable and retractable options embedded in debt issues.

Callable debt combines the debt component, which would otherwise not be callable, with the call provision, which provides a call option to the issuer. A callable security contains a provision that allows the issuer to retire the security a given price (call price). If interest rates decline, the issuer can retire the higher-interest debt through the use of the call provision and subsequently reissue lower-interest debt. Normally a minimum period of time is required before the bond can be called away. The issuer typically incurs a cost for the call option

Call Schedule

A fixed income instrument may have a call schedule consisting of several call dates and prices throughout its life. Typically, call prices compensate the investor for lost income, with higher call prices for earlier calls. A portion of a call schedule may show, for example:

Callable at 101.50	Jun 16, 2009
Callable at 101.00	Jun 16, 2010
Callable at 100.50	Jun 16, 2011
Callable at par	Thereafter with 30 days' notice

through the call price schedule and higher interest payments to investors.

New reporting and accounting rules affect embedded options in debt securities. These rules are discussed briefly in Chapter 8.

A retractable bond includes a provision that allows the investor to redeem it with the issuer at a specified price, providing the investor with protection if market interest rates rise. The retractable issue provides protection for the investor but not the issuer, although the issuer may be able to pay a lower rate of interest to the investor.

Enhanced Cash Flow Management

Better cash flow management may permit an organization to maintain cash balances for longer periods of time. This can reduce the need for funding and therefore exposure to interest rates, particularly in countries or currencies with less liquidity or additional difficulty moving funds. Some of these techniques may be helpful in improving cash flows:

- Effective use of accounts payable, including reevaluation of credit terms and policies and tightening collection from slow payors.

- Changes to customer payment schedules may increase the speed with which funds are collected, reducing reliance on borrowing.

- Changes to payment methods used by customers, such as encouraging electronic alternatives to paper checks, may also speed collections and make cash flow forecasts more reliable.

Asset-Liability Management

Asset-liability management involves the matching of assets and liabilities so that interest rate exposure is minimized, reducing the potential adverse impact on the organization. In a financial institution, asset-liability management involves matching customer loans or mortgages, for example, with customer deposits. In a nonfinancial institution, this might mean matching funding (e.g., long term) with long-term assets (e.g., plant expansion).

Matching may be conducted on a maturity basis or, to better reflect interest rate sensitivity, with measures such as duration. Where cash needs to be raised, securitization of assets, such as mortgages or receivables, may help improve liquidity and reduce the need for funding. Securitization is discussed in more detail in Chapter 3.

Some nonfinancial companies have exposure to interest rate mismatches through financing programs for their customers or internal financing for projects. Nonfinancial institutions may be able to reduce interest rate exposure by building an awareness of asset-liability management within parts of the organization involved in such activities and using it to reduce exposure where possible.

Interest Rate Basics

Yield Curve

The yield curve is the graphical representation of interest rates for various terms to maturity, from overnight (1 day) to 30 years, for example. The yield for any particular maturity is found as a point along the yield curve. Yields are normally zero-coupon rates, without the distortion effect of coupon payments.

In a normal interest rate environment, longer-term interest rates are higher than shorter-term interest rates. This difference compensates the lender for the additional risks associated with a longer lending term to maturity. As a result, the yield curve usually has an upward sloping appearance.

The shape of the yield curve suggests something about the market's anticipation of future interest rates. Forward interest rates are interest rates for periods of time beginning at a future date, and they can be derived from the yield curve. An upward-sloping yield curve suggests that market participants expect rates to rise. Conversely, a downward-sloping yield curve suggests that market participants expect rates to fall.

Interest Rate Basis

The management of interest rate exposure necessarily requires consideration of interest rate basis. Due to the attributes of the market, the

Libor and Euribor

Libor (London Interbank Offered Rate) is a widely used benchmark or reference rate for short-term U.S. dollar interest rates. Libor is the interbank rate between major banks for transactions of market size. It is calculated daily by the British Bankers Association from rates posted by a group of active contributor banks. Libor is used for settlement of many interest rate derivatives contracts and lending arrangements.

Libor rates are posted daily for British pound, Japanese yen, Canadian dollar, Australian dollar, euro, Danish krone, New Zealand dollar, Swiss franc, and U.S. dollar for maturities up to 12 months.

Euribor (*www.euribor.org*) is the Euro interbank offered rate, which is the lending rate for prime banks. It is posted by the European Banking Federation and the Financial Markets Association (ACI, or Association Cambiste Internationale). Euribor differs from Eurepo, which is a repo (secured) rate for collateral consisting of government bonds and bills issued by euro countries. The banks that comprise the calculation of Euribor differ from the Eurepo panel of banks.[1]

yield curve, and credit quality, all interest rates do not change simultaneously. For example, the bank prime rate is an administered rate and can remain unchanged although market rates fluctuate significantly.

When there is a mismatch between the exposure being hedged and the transaction used for hedging purposes, an organization may not have adequate reduction of interest rate risk. Using one interest rate product to hedge another type of interest rate exposure may be an alternative for an effective hedge at reasonable cost. However, if there is an incomplete match between the hedge and the exposure, the organization should consider the opportunity for loss.

Forward Rate Agreements

A forward rate agreement (FRA) is an over-the-counter agreement between two parties, a notional borrower and a notional lender, to lock in an interest rate for a short period of time. The period is typically one month or three months, beginning at a future date. The notional nature is important because the contract amount itself does not change hands between the counterparties.

A borrower buys an FRA to protect against rising interest rates, while a lender sells an FRA to protect against declining interest rates. Counterparties to an FRA can continue to borrow or invest through normal channels. The FRA provides interest rate protection against changes in rates as measured by the reference rate specified in the contract. Rates being hedged should be the same or similar to the FRA reference rate to avoid basis risk.

At the beginning of the period covered by the FRA, the settlement reference rate is compared to the FRA rate. If the reference rate is higher, the FRA seller pays a compensating payment (the settlement amount) to the FRA buyer. If the reference rate is lower, the FRA buyer pays the settlement amount to the FRA seller. The notional contract amount is used for calculating the settlement amount.

The following terminology applies to FRAs:

- The forward term of an FRA is the time prior to the beginning of the FRA.

- The contract term is the time covered by the FRA.

- The settlement rate is the reference rate on the settlement date.

- FRA reference rates are posted on major market information services, commonly Libor or BA rates.

- The settlement amount is the payment to the FRA seller or buyer, based on the differential between the reference rate and the FRA rate at the beginning of the contract period, prorated over the term of the FRA.

- The maturity date of the FRA is the end of the contract term.

Although payment of the settlement amount usually occurs at the beginning of the contract term, it can occur at the end of the contract term. If payment occurs at the beginning of the contract term, the settlement amount that would otherwise be paid is discounted at current rates and the present value of the interest rate differential is paid.

Closing out an FRA contract involves unwinding it through an offsetting transaction. The buyer of an FRA will sell an offsetting FRA, while the seller of an FRA will buy an offsetting FRA, with a resultant profit or loss.

Interest Rate Futures

Interest rate futures are exchange-traded forwards. They permit an organization to manage exposure to interest rates or fixed income prices by locking in a price or rate for a future time period. Futures contracts are transacted through a broker, and there are transaction commissions and margin requirements.

FRA Rates

FRA rates are forward interest rates and are determined by the yield curve. They effectively allow the yield curve to be split into small segments that can be hedged or traded independently of one another. FRA rates are shown in a standard format with time to beginning of contract term and time to end of contract term, usually in months, for example:

FRA Term	FRA Rate
1 x 4 months	3.55 – 3.60%
2 x 5	3.75 – 3.80%
3 x 6	3.95 – 4.00%

A borrower wanting to protect against rising rates beginning in three months' time and ending in six months' time could buy an FRA from the listed rates at 4.00% (the offered side of the 3 × 6 price quote). The term 3 × 6 indicates that the FRA term begins three months from the trade date and ends six months from the trade date.

A strip of consecutive FRAs can be used to construct a longer-term hedge. For example, a one-year hedge could be constructed using consecutive three-month FRAs.

Interest rate futures contracts do not require the establishment of a line of credit with a bank. The risk of dealing with other counterparties is replaced with exposure to the exchange clearinghouse.

The underlying asset for an interest rate futures contract may be a benchmark interest rate, composite index, or fixed income instrument. For example, in the case of a bond futures contract, the futures

IN THE REAL WORLD

Calculating an FRA Settlement Amount

A company needs to borrow $10 million in three months' time. Management is concerned that rates may rise, so the company buys a 3 × 6 FRA at 4.00 percent with a term of three months, or 90 days.

If interest rates have risen (as measured by the reference rate compared with the FRA rate), the bank will compensate the company. If the reference rate has fallen, the company will compensate the bank.

FRA rate	4.00%
Reference (actual) rate	5.00%
Difference	1.00%

1.00% × 90 days/360 days* × $10 million = $25,000

Since the settlement amount usually is paid at the beginning of the period covered by the FRA, the amount is discounted and its present value paid ($24,691.36).

*Note: The daycount basis in many countries, including the United States, is 360 days. Canada and several other countries use 365 days. It is the method used to calculate number of days for purposes of settlement or interest amounts.

price locks in the price for the bond and the resultant yield, since prices and yields move inversely.

As with other forwards, locking in a price for the underlying asset or an interest rate through a futures contract also means forfeiting the possibility of subsequent favorable market moves.

Short-term Interest Rate Futures

Short-term interest rate (STIR) futures trade on several ex-changes, including the Chicago Board of Trade, the International Monetary Market (IMM) division of the Chicago Mercantile Ex-change, and the Montreal Exchange. These contracts permit users to fix a price for the underlying instrument and therefore the corre-sponding interest rate, or alternatively fix the interest rate directly.

For many years the IMM Eurodollar futures contract was the most active U.S. short-term interest rate futures contract. Eu-rodollars are U.S. dollar bank deposits held outside the United States. They are actively traded and often used for arbitrage ac-tivities in the foreign exchange forward markets.

A Eurodollar futures contract locks in a price and the corre-sponding interest rate on $1 million. Eurodollar futures quotes are price indices from which interest rates are determined and cash settled. For example, the December rate is 100 – 97.66, or 2.34%. Sample three-month Eurodollar rates, traded on the Chicago Mercantile Exchange, are:

Dec	97.66
Mar	97.42
Jun	97.23
Sep	97.04

Basis risk is a consideration when contracts used differ from the organization's exposure—for example, exposure to an administered borrowing rate hedged with a Eurodollar contract.

TIPS & TECHNIQUES

Futures Strips

A strip of futures contracts can also be used to construct a hedge for a longer period of time. The result is similar to an interest rate swap, where consecutive contracts together cover a longer period of time, such as one year. The strategy is limited by the maximum expiry dates of the contracts available.

Futures Margin

The futures user must post margin (cash or similar securities) in an account maintained by the broker who facilitated the transaction. Minimum margin is set by the exchange, and brokers may require additional margin.

Margin is a performance bond to ensure that the buyer or seller of a futures contract fulfills the obligations associated with the contract. Outstanding futures positions are marked-to-market daily, and the margin account of the futures buyer or seller is debited or credited accordingly. By preventing unrealized losses from accumulating, margin helps to safeguard the clearinghouse and the financial system.

Margin is designed to absorb potential subsequent losses on the open futures position. The amount of margin required depends on exchange rules and whether the position is hedging or speculative. Failure to respond to a margin call may lead the broker to close out the futures position by offsetting the contracts outstanding at the account holder's cost.

Bond Futures

Bond futures can be used to hedge bond and interest rate risk, change portfolio asset allocation, or alter portfolio duration, without buying or selling the underlying bonds. They are useful for tactical asset allocation strategies employed by professional money and portfolio managers. In addition, they can assist in the management of exposure to long-term interest rates.

A borrower can protect against rising interest rates (falling prices) by selling a bond futures contract provided that the underlying interest is similar to the exposure. If interest rates rise (underlying bond price falls), the gain on the futures contract should offset higher market interest rates. If interest rates fall (underlying bond price rises), the loss on the futures contracts should offset lower market interest rates. This presumes that there has been no change in the willingness of the organization's lenders to extend credit.

Basis risk can impact the ultimate effectiveness of the hedge and is a consideration in interest rate futures, particularly bond futures, because many are based on government debt. Also, the underlying (cheapest-to-deliver) bond can change during the term of a futures contract.

Even if the futures contract provides a hedge against market interest rates, as measured by the underlying asset, it does not address other issues, such as the deterioration of the user's credit quality, which is also a risk factor. In most cases, the credit quality of the user will differ from that of the contract's underlying issuer.

Bond futures are useful in portfolio management for facilitating tactical and strategic asset allocation. A portfolio manager can alter asset weightings by buying or selling futures contracts without changing actual holdings of securities. The advantages of using bond futures as a proxy to actual purchases of bonds include ease of execution and delivery and potential for reduced transaction costs.

TIPS & TECHNIQUES

Hedge Ratios

Futures contracts trade in standardized contract amounts and for standardized underlying assets. A hedge ratio helps to determine the number of contracts needed to ensure an effective hedge against exposure, provided that the contract is appropriate for the underlying exposure. An incorrect number of contracts can mean under- or overhedging. Hedge ratio adjustments are estimates and therefore inexact.

Hedge ratios reflect price sensitivities. The goal of hedging is to match a change in the exposure (e.g., bond portfolio) with an off-setting change in the value of a hedge (e.g., futures contract). To determine a hedge ratio, the rate of change of the futures contract is compared with the rate of change of the underlying exposure (although they will be in different directions).

A basic ratio is calculated by dividing nominal exposure by nominal futures contract size. This ratio can be used if the underlying exposure is the same as the futures contract. Otherwise, if the exposure to be hedged differs from the futures contract, the basic ratio can be adjusted. Adjustments may be based on the ratio of basis point values, the correlation between the two interest rates or assets, or another calculation.

Exchanges that list bond futures provide a list of bonds that meet delivery requirements. The cheapest-to-deliver bond is the most favorable for the bond seller to deliver, producing the greatest profit or the smallest loss, within delivery requirements. Bond futures prices track the cheapest-to-deliver bond, which itself can change during the futures contract's lifetime. The conversion factor of the cheapest-to-deliver bond, or alternatively duration, may be used to develop a hedge ratio.

continued on next page

TIPS & TECHNIQUES CONTINUED

The hedge ratio may need further adjusting if the exposure differs from the cheapest-to-deliver bond. Historical price data or regression analysis can also be used to develop a hedge ratio. However, relationships between instruments can change and may differ from the historical period tracked. It is for this reason that hedge ratios are an estimate of the number of contracts required.

Closing Out a Futures Contract

At expiry, a futures contract can be settled by offsetting it with another futures contract or by delivering or accepting delivery of the underlying, as permitted by the terms of the contract. For delivery against bond futures contracts, because deliverable bonds have different coupons and maturities, a conversion factor is used. Exchanges list deliverable bonds and their conversion factors.

Prior to delivery, a purchased futures contract can be closed out by selling a futures contract with the same delivery date. Similarly, a sold futures contract can be offset by buying a futures contract with the same delivery date.

Commonly, futures contracts are rolled forward to maintain the position. This is accomplished by closing out the near-term delivery contract (buying or selling) and entering into a new contract with farther delivery date (selling or buying).

Interest Rate Swaps

Interest rate swaps are bilateral negotiated contracts that enable two parties to exchange their respective interest rate obligations. The swap exists independently of any debt or investment. Most commonly, the swap involves a fixed rate payment exchanged for a floating rate payment (or vice versa). However, swaps can be highly customized and may contain embedded option features that add complexity to their analysis.

Transacted in the over-the-counter market, interest rate swaps are related to forwards and futures but facilitate interest rate hedging over a longer time interval. Common swaps include asset swaps, basis swaps, zero-coupon swaps, and forward interest rate swaps.

Swaps permit a change to the effective nature of an asset or liability without changing the underlying exposure. For example, payment structures can be changed in anticipation of rising interest rates. Alternatively, organizations may be able to take advantage of benefits, such as government or tax incentives, that are available for certain types of financing, such as long-term financing.

Borrowers with weaker credit ratings normally face a credit premium for fixed rate borrowing. Such an organization may borrow at relatively more attractive floating rates and swap for the desired fixed rate payments without any change to the underlying debt.

Asset Swaps

A swap to transform an asset's income stream is known as an asset swap. Asset swaps allow investors to change the interest rate structure of their revenue streams without changing the structure of the underlying asset. Both interest rate swaps and currency swaps can be asset swaps.

The most popular asset swaps are those that change payments from a fixed interest rate to a floating interest rate and those that exchange a cash flow in one currency to another currency.

TIPS & TECHNIQUES

Swap Counterparties

The principal notional (contractual) amount of an interest rate swap is not exchanged between counterparties but is used to calculate payments. Due to the fact that only net cash flows are exchanged between counterparties, credit exposure is reduced. However, swaps often have large notional contract amounts and significant terms to maturity, which means the credit quality of counterparties should be monitored. High-quality counterparties should be chosen.

The terms receiver and payor refer to the fixed rate payment stream in a swap. The benchmark floating rate is, by convention, an average from several market-making financial institutions. Rates are posted on major financial information services. This convention helps avoid contention over the correct benchmark or opportunities for manipulation. Three- or six-month Libor are common benchmark floating rates. Master agreements are provided by the International Swaps and Derivatives Association (ISDA).

When interest rates are expected to fall, market participants move to floating interest rates, and there is downward pressure on swap spreads. When interest rates are expected to rise, market participants will move to borrow at fixed interest rates, putting upward pressure on swap spreads.

Asset swaps can also be used to synthetically create a return that would not otherwise be available. For example, consider an investment that offers a floating rate return at a relatively attractive price. An investor that prefers fixed rate assets can buy the floating rate asset and swap the revenue stream for a fixed rate revenue stream without changing the structure of the asset.

IN THE REAL WORLD

Swap Rates

Swap spreads, and therefore all-in swap rates, fluctuate in response to supply and demand. The spread is added to the benchmark (government) yield for the fixed rate. A financial institution will pay fixed at the bid rate or receive fixed at the offered rate.

Term of Swap	Governments	Spreads	All-in Rate (Bank Bid-Offer)
2 years	4.40–4.45	20–25	4.60–4.70
3 years	4.60–4.65	25–30	4.85–4.95
4 years	4.70–4.75	25–30	4.95–5.05
5 years	4.95–5.00	25–30	5.20–5.30

A corporate borrower wanting to exchange floating rate payments for fixed rate payments (pay fixed and receive floating) for five years will pay an all-in swap rate of 5.30 (5.00 + .30) percent from the sample swap rates and spreads shown.

Similarly, an investor with foreign currency assets may prefer U.S. dollar revenues that offset a need for U.S. dollars elsewhere in the business. The investor could swap the foreign currency revenues for U.S. dollar revenues without affecting the foreign assets.

Interest Rate Options

The two basic types of options are puts and calls. A call option on interest rates provides protection to the option buyer from rising rates,

Terminating a Swap

To be terminated, an interest rate swap must be settled at market value. The market value of a swap at any time after its commencement is the net present value of future remaining cash flows. Swap termination involves the calculation of a settlement amount representing the net present value of all future obligations by each counterparty. This net payment is made to the counterparty disadvantaged by the termination of the swap.

There are several ways to alter or eliminate an existing interest rate swap:

- Offset the swap with another that will produce the required payment streams.

- Cancel the existing swap by paying or receiving a lump sum representing the net present value of remaining payments. If the swap has a negative value, a cash payment may be required.

- Extend the swap by blending it with a new one (blend-and-extend). This embeds the cost of closing out the swap in the new periodic swap payments.

- Assign the swap to another party that will continue to make and receive payments under the original swap agreement until maturity. The counterparty assigning the swap will either pay to or receive from the new counterparty a lump sum that reflects the net present value of all remaining payment streams.

as defined by the reference rate. A put option on interest rates provides protection to the option buyer from declining rates, as defined by the reference rate. The reference rate is set out in the option contract as the benchmark against which the potential benefits to the option buyer are measured.

The business of options is analogous to insurance. One party pays to reduce or eliminate risk, while the other party accepts the risk in exchange for option premium. Option premium paid increases the effective borrowing cost, or decreases the effective return on assets, for hedgers.

Although the mechanics are similar, the contractual details of an interest rate option are important because the underlying interest may be specific interest rates, a fixed income security such as a government bond, swap contract, or futures contract. The user should clearly understand the contractual details to judge the appropriateness of the option as a hedge, given the organization's own exposure and objectives.

The interest rate option contract details include:

- Strike price, which is the interest rate that the option buyer is permitted to borrow or lend funds (in the case of an option on interest rates)

- Reference rate, which is the applicable interest rate specified in the contract, or underlying fixed income security

- Expiry, which is the date the option contract, if not exercised, expires

- Contract or notional amount, which is the amount of funds that can be borrowed or lent under the terms of the contract

(or alternatively, the amount of a fixed income security that can be purchased or sold)

- Exercise, which is the use of the contract by the option buyer, including how and when it can be exercised, whether it is cash-settled or settled by delivery of the underlying asset, and, if permitted, delivery opportunities

Common interest rate option strategies include caps, floors, and collars used to protect against specific reference interest rates or underlying asset prices. Although option strategies usually involve over-the-counter options, they can also be constructed from exchange-traded options.

Options on fixed income securities or futures contracts may differ slightly and trade based on the security rather than the associated interest rate, as yields and fixed income prices move inversely. For such contracts, a call option gives the option buyer right to buy the security (protection against rising prices and falling rates), while a put option gives the option buyer the right to sell the security (protection against falling prices and rising rates).

Pricing of interest rate options depends on several factors, including term to expiry, strike rate, and volatility of the reference interest rate. Prices normally are quoted in basis points of the notional contract amount. The option buyer's specification for contract size, strike rate, reset dates, term to expiry, and reference interest rate can be customized in the over-the-counter market.

Purchased interest rate options can be costly if the underlying rate is volatile. If underlying rates move, but not enough to make the option worth exercising, the option will expire worthless, resulting in a potential loss through adverse market rates as well as the cost of the option premium.

Caps and Floors

Caps and floors are interest rate options packaged to provide protection from changes in interest rates over a period of time. A cap is a series of interest rate options to protect against rising interest rates. A cap (sometimes called a ceiling) is typically made up of short European-style options, the expiry of each option corresponding to the hedger's anticipated borrowing schedule. In exchange for cap premium, the cap buyer is protected from higher rates (above the cap strike rate) for the period of time covered by the cap.

At the expiry date of each individual option (caplet), the cap seller reimburses the cap buyer if the reference rate is above the cap strike rate. If rates are below the cap rate, the caplet is left to expire, and funding can be obtained at lower market rates. Unexpired portions of the cap (caplets) remain for future borrowing dates.

Example: Interest Rate Cap

A U.S. manufacturer borrows by rolling over short-term debt every quarter. Concerned about rising rates, the company buys an interest rate cap to cover its $10 million floating rate debt. The cap strike rate is 5.00 percent, the reset period is quarterly to match the debt rate resets, and the reference rate is the Libor rate on the reset date. One potential scenario follows.

Rollover 1   At the first rollover and cap date, the average reference rate is 4.25 percent. The company will do nothing, since the reference rate is lower than the cap rate. The company will borrow at the lower market rates, and the cap will remain for subsequent rollover dates until its expiry.

Rollover 2 At the second rollover and cap date, the rate has increased to 5.65 percent. The company will be reim-
bursed by its bank for the difference between the
cap strike rate and the reference rate. Assuming 91
days in the period, this amount is calculated as

$$\frac{\$10,000,000 \times (0.0565 - 0.0500) \times 91}{360} = \$16,430.56.$$

Compensation to the cap buyer is based on the difference between
the strike rate and the reference rate for the notional contract amount
and the period of time covered by the option. Although the cost of the
cap increases the effective cost of funds for a borrower, it also provides
protection and flexibility without locking in a rate.

A floor is similar to a cap except that it provides protection against
falling rates below the floor strike rate. A floor provides the floor buyer
with reimbursement if the reference rate falls below the floor strike rate.

As an alternative to buying a cap, a borrower may sell an interest rate
floor, receiving the floor premium. The borrower will be required to pay
the floor rate should the floor be exercised by the floor buyer. The floor
will be exercised only if interest rates fall. The floor premium received will
partially offset higher borrowing costs, but the floor seller still incurs all
the risk of rising interest rates and has not hedged against higher rates.

Collars

An interest rate collar comprises a cap and a floor, one purchased and
one sold. Collars often are used when caps (or floors) are deemed too
expensive. The purchased option provides protection against adverse
interest rate movements. The sold option trades away some of the benefits of favorable rates in order to pay for the protective option. Like

caps and floors, collars typically consist of a series of interest rate options with expiry dates customized to the hedger's schedule.

If, at expiry of each option comprising the collar, the reference rate is between the cap and floor rates, neither the cap nor the floor will be exercised. However, if rates move above the cap rate or below the floor rate, the appropriate option (cap or floor) will be exercised.

Effectively, rates will be capped at the cap rate or prevented from falling below the floor rate. If the reference interest rate moves beyond strike rate, the option is exercised and the option seller pays the option buyer the difference between the reference rate and the strike rate on the notional amount, adjusted for the number of days in that option's term.

Collars may be transacted independently of the underlying exposure they are designed to hedge. In a zero-cost collar, option premiums offset one another. Like other interest rate options, the collar protects against changing market interest rates but does not provide protection against rate changes as a result of the deterioration of a borrower's credit.

Swaptions

Swaptions are options on interest rate swaps. They give the swaption buyer the right, but not the obligation, to enter into an interest rate swap with predetermined characteristics at the option's expiry. Swaption premium is paid by the swaption buyer to the swaption seller, typically as a percentage of the notional amount of the swap.

An interest rate swaption has the effect of locking in a fixed interest rate (or, alternatively, a floating interest rate). For example, in anticipation of rising interest rates, a swaption buyer can exercise its option to enter into a pay-fixed (receive floating) swap, providing protection against higher rates. The cost of such a strategy is the swaption premium.

The terms receiver and payor refer to the fixed rate payment stream in a swap:

- The buyer of a payor swaption has the right to enter a pay-fixed (receive floating) swap at the strike rate.

- The buyer of a receiver swaption has the right to enter a receive-fixed (pay floating) swap at the strike rate.

A floating rate borrower can purchase a swaption giving it the right, but not the obligation, to enter into an interest rate swap at the expiry of the swaption. In exchange for this right, the buyer of the swaption pays a premium.

Swaptions may also be sold to earn premium income that can be used to reduce interest costs. The swaption seller takes on potentially unlimited risk because the swaption will be exercised only when the current market is less favorable (to the swaption seller) than the swap strike rate. The swaption seller must be comfortable entering into a swap with the specified terms or, alternatively, not having the swaption exercised.

For the swaption seller, the swaption premium is the only offset for the risk undertaken. The swaption seller may be obligated to enter into the underlying swap, or pay to exit from the obligation, if the swaption is exercisable at expiry. The sale of a swaption alone also does nothing to hedge interest rate exposure.

Exchange-Traded Options

Exchange-traded options may have a futures contract as the underlying interest. Options on interest rates or options on interest rate futures can be used to construct an interest rate cap, floor, or collar. Options may be settled in cash or with the underlying asset or futures contract, depending on exchange rules. Basis risk may be a consideration if exchange-traded options are used for hedging purposes.

When the underlying interest is a futures contract, the purchase of a put option permits the option buyer to sell the futures contract at the strike price, which provides protection against falling (futures) prices. The purchase of a call option on a futures contract allows the option buyer to buy the futures contract at the strike price, providing protection against rising (futures) prices.

Closing Out an Interest Rate Option

In general, if an interest rate option is no longer required and there is time remaining to expiry, it can be sold at market value. For a strategy involving several purchased options, market value is the total of the options that comprise it, and the maximum loss is the cost of the options, in addition to any losses as a result of an organization's exposure.

A sold option remains an obligation to the option seller unless it has been closed out by purchasing an offsetting one and the outstanding option is canceled. Interest rate collars and other strategies that comprise both purchased and sold options involve such potential obligations.

Sold options with time and/or intrinsic value may be expensive to repurchase. Therefore, the maximum loss may be greater than the original cost (for a package of bought and sold options) or premium received (for sold options).

An option will be worthless if there is no intrinsic value at expiry. Some exchange-traded contracts offer automatic exercise on options that are in-the-money by a certain minimum amount, while others require the option buyer to notify in case of exercise.

At a swaption's expiry, if it is not favorable to use it, the swaption buyer can allow it to expire and transact a swap at market rates. If the swaption is favorable, the swaption buyer can exercise it and enter into the predetermined swap. Alternatively, an in-the-money swaption may be sold, or alternatively closed out with a difference payment from the swaption seller to the swaption buyer.

Summary

- Basic changes to the way that business is conducted may help to minimize an organization's exposure to interest rates.

- Forward rate agreements (FRAs) and futures contracts permit a rate to be fixed for a specific period of time, while swaps permit a hedge to be constructed for a longer period of time.

- A hedge ratio helps to determine the number of exchange-traded contracts needed to ensure an effective hedge. An incorrect number of contracts can result in under- or overhedging.

- Interest rate caps and floors provide hedgers with protection against rising (or falling) rates, without locking in an interest rate.

Note

1. Hanspeter K. Scheller, *The European Central Bank* (European Central Bank, 2004).

CHAPTER 6

Treasury Risks

After reading this chapter, you should be able to:

- Discuss different types of risks facing an organization's treasury.
- Understand how financial risks arise.
- Identify methods to assess exposure and risk.

Introduction

Organizations face many risks. Risks arise from every activity of an organization. The process of risk assessment is a method to determine the priorities and risk control required within an organization. The risks included here are those typically managed or assessed by the treasury department. The major treasury-related risks include:

- Market risks arising from market prices and rates (e.g., from purchases, sales, funding)

- Credit risks arising from commercial and financial market activities

- Operational risks that involve people, processes, or systems

- Liquidity risks that involve an organization's ability to prevent depletion of financial assets and the risks and returns on invested assets

Interest Rate Risk

Interest rate risk includes absolute interest rate risk, yield curve risk, and reinvestment or refunding risk. Risks arising from embedded options are also a consideration.

Absolute Interest Rate Risk

Absolute interest rate risk arises from exposure to a directional (up or down) change in interest rates. Most organizations monitor absolute interest rate risk closely as part of their risk assessments, due to its visibility and potential for affecting profitability.

Yield Curve Risk

Yield curve risk results from changes in the relationship between short- and long-term interest rates. In a normal interest rate environment, the yield curve has an upward-sloping shape to it. Longer-term interest rates are higher than shorter-term interest rates because of higher risk to the lender. The steepening or flattening of the yield curve changes the interest rate differential between maturities, which can impact borrowing and investment decisions and therefore profitability.

Reinvestment or Refunding Risk

Reinvestment or refunding risk arises when investment maturities (or debt maturities) occur during periods of unfavorable interest rates. As a result, funds are reinvested (or debt refinanced) at market rates that are worse than forecast, impacting profitability. The inability to forecast the rollover rate with certainty has the potential to impact overall profitability of the investment or project. Reinvestment or refunding risk is closely related to absolute interest rate risk but applies to a specific future requirement.

Embedded Options Risk

Embedded options provide securities holders or contract participants with rights that can introduce risk to the granting party. For example, the ability to repay a loan prior to its maturity is an option. If the loan can be repaid without a fee, then the granting party has a risk that the loan will be paid at an inopportune time.

Foreign Exchange Risk

Foreign exchange risk arises through various sources, including transactions, translation of financial statements, and the activities of competitors. Foreign exchange issues are discussed in more detail in Chapter 4.

Transaction Risk

Transaction risk arises from transactions reported in an organization's income statement. It exists as a result of purchases of inventory from suppliers and vendors, contractual payments, royalties or license fees, and sales to customers in currencies other than the domestic one. Organizations that buy or sell products and services denominated in a foreign currency, including companies with operations or subsidiaries in other countries, typically are exposed to transaction risk.

Translation Risk

Translation risk traditionally referred to risk that arose from the accounting translation of assets and liabilities for financial statement purposes. Translation risk can result when assets, liabilities, or profits are translated from the operating currency into a reporting currency—for example, the reporting currency of a parent company.

Strategic Risk

Strategic risk, sometimes called economic risk, arises from the location and activities of major competitors. When foreign exchange rates change, it may provide competitors with an advantage, depending on the currencies in which their business is denominated. Strategic risk thus has the potential to affect an organization's competitive position and market share as a result of changes in exchange rates. These risks may not be visible on the balance sheet, although their impact appears in the income statement.

Commodity Risk

Commodities differ from financial contracts in several significant ways, primarily due to the fact that most have the potential to involve physical delivery. With notable exceptions, such as electricity, commodities involve issues such as quality, delivery location, transportation, spoilage, shortages, and storability, and these issues affect price and trading activity. Commodity risks include price and quantity risk.

Commodity Price Risk

Commodity price risk is the probability of changes in the price of a commodity that is a component of an organization's business. Typically, price risk arises from products that must be purchased or sold, but it can also arise indirectly through prices that are themselves affected by commodity prices. Commodity exposure can also arise from noncommodity business if inputs or products and services have a commodity component. Commodity price risk affects consumers and end users such as manufacturers, governments, processors, and wholesalers. It may be managed by treasury or by another group within the organization that focuses specifically on the commodity component.

Commodity Quantity Risk

Quantity risk arises through the requirement for commodity assets or the ability to sell adequate quantity. Although quantity is closely tied to price, quantity risk remains an issue because supply and demand are critical with respect to commodities in production or operations.

Credit Risk

Credit risk is prevalent throughout the world of business. Many organizations extend trade credit, use derivatives, and borrow. Credit risk is a major concern when an organization is owed money or relies on other organizations to pay or make a payment on its behalf. However, depending on the legal environment and whether funds are owed on a net or aggregate or individual basis can also affect credit risk. In addition, the deterioration of a borrower's credit quality is also a source of credit risk through the reduced ability to issue debt or borrow. Credit risk also arises through holding of debt securities issued by another organization.

Default Risk

Default risk arises from the default of funds owed either through lending or investment. The borrower may be unable or unwilling to repay. In many cases, the default amount is most or all of the advanced funds, unless a partial recovery is possible.

Counterparty Risk

Counterparty risk arises from the performance of counterparties to contractual arrangements, such as derivatives. Counterparty risk exists during both the settlement process and the presettlement period. Settlement risk, in particular, is a key market risk that market participants and regulators have worked to reduce.

Prior to settlement, in the presettlement period, if a counterparty defaults or otherwise fails to fulfill its obligations, it might be necessary to enter into a replacement contract at far less favorable prices.

During the settlement process, counterparty risk is particularly important. Settlement risk arises at the time that payments associated with a contract occur, particularly cross-payments between counterparties. It has the potential to result in large losses because the entire amount of the payment between counterparties may be at risk if a counterparty fails during the settlement process.

Sovereign or Country Risk

Certain transactions expose an organization to the rules and discretion of foreign governments. Sovereign risk encompasses the legal, regulatory, and political exposures that encompass international transactions and the movement of funds across borders, for example. It arises through the actions of foreign governments and countries. When issues occur, they can have significant financial impact. Exposure to nondomestic organizations necessarily involves an analysis of the associated sovereign risk, particularly in areas with political instability.

Concentration Risk

Concentration risk is a source of credit risk that arises from credit exposure in concentrated sectors. Many organizations are poorly diversified, due to their industry or regional influences. Although concentration risk can be managed for certain components of an organization's business, such as the investment portfolio, in other areas it may be much more difficult to avoid. For example, many organizations become successful by concentrating their efforts in key industry, regional, or product areas where they have the greatest strengths.

Legal Risk

Legal risk arises from the possibility that a counterparty is not legally permitted or able to enter into transactions, particularly derivatives transactions. The issue of legal risk has arisen in the past after a counterparty suffered losses on outstanding derivatives contracts. A related issue is the legal structure of the counterparty to a transaction, since many derivatives counterparties, for example, are wholly-owned special-purpose subsidiaries.

Operational Risk

Operational risk arises from human error and fraud, processes and procedures, and technology and systems. Operational risk is one of the most significant risks facing an organization due to the varied opportunities for losses to occur and the fact that losses may be substantial when they occur. Operational risks often are interrelated. For example, a weakness that permits an electronic funds transfer to occur fraudulently may be related to personnel (human error and fraud), technology (technology and systems risk), and process.

Human Error and Fraud

Most business transactions involve human decision making and relationships. A small percentage of transactions are fraudulent or erroneous. However, the size and volume of financial transactions in organizations make the potential damage as a result of error or fraud significant. The subject of fraud is complex and relatively specialized and is beyond the scope of this book. However, it highlights the necessity of effective internal audit and control procedures and the importance of selecting and maintaining a well-trained and ethical workforce.

Processes and Procedural Risk

Risks arising from processes and procedures include adverse consequences through missing, or ineffective controls, or checks and balances. The use of inadequate controls is an example of a procedural risk. Attempts to manage these risks have come under scrutiny through legislation such as the Sarbanes-Oxley Act in the United States.

Technology and Systems Risk

Weaknesses in technology and systems provide opportunities for errors, failures, lost data, and fraud, among other things. Technology and systems risks arise as a result of the systems that support an organization's transactions and business.

Liquidity Risk

Liquidity risk is a major, prevalent risk. The ability of an organization to maintain adequate liquidity through its management of cash and working capital is critical to its survival. Liquidity risk is the risk that an organization has the financial capacity to meet its short-term obligations.

Liquidity risk can also refer to the ability or cost associated with buying or selling securities or closing out contracts, for either hedging or trading purposes. Liquidity, which can change quickly, impacts all markets. The less liquid a market is, the more difficult and costly it will be to undertake transactions in that market.

Other Risks

Other risks include basis risk, equity price risk, systemic risk, and reputation risk. These are risks that the treasury professional should be aware of, but they are not all part of the normal day-to-day functions of treasury. In addition, there are many other risks that have not been mentioned.

Basis Risk

Basis risk is the risk that a hedge, such as a derivatives contract, does not adequately provide protection against a market move. It may not

IN THE REAL WORLD

Reputation Risk

Given the importance of trust and integrity in the business of banking, reputation risk is a critical component of financial institution risk management. The Office of the Superintendent of Financial Institutions (OSFI) regulates banks in Canada, as well as some nonbank financial institutions. In June 2005, it published *Review of Reputation Risk Practices: Principles, Observations, and Next Steps,* covering basic principles, observations, and issues associated with reputation risk management. These issues include the identification of reputation risk management as an important aspect of an effective risk management framework, senior management and board oversight, effective reputation risk policies, reputation risk management training programs to increase employee awareness and ability to identify and manage reputation risk, and internal audit. The document can be read on the OSFI web site (*www.osfi.gc.ca*).

move in the same direction or magnitude as the underlying exposure, and it is a concern whenever there is a mismatch between exposure and hedge. Basis risk may occur when one hedging product is used as a proxy hedge for the underlying exposure, possibly because an appropriate hedge is expensive or impossible to find.

Equity Price Risk

Equity price risk affects corporate investors with equities or other assets, the performance of which is tied to equity prices. Firms may have equity exposure through pension fund investments, for example, where the return depends on a stream of dividends and favorable equity price movements to provide capital gains. The exposure may be to one stock, several stocks, or an industry or the market as a whole.

Equity price risk also affects companies' ability to fund operations through the sale of equity and equity-related securities. Equity risk is thus related to the ability of a firm to obtain sufficient working capital or liquidity.

Systemic Risk

Systemic risk is the risk that the failure of a major financial institution could trigger a domino effect and many subsequent organizational failures, threatening the integrity of the global financial system. Aside from practicing good risk management principles, systemic risk is difficult for an individual organization to mitigate. Higher volumes, especially for foreign exchange and securities trading, increase liquidity but also increase systemic risk. Systemic risk can also arise from technological failure or a major disaster.

IN THE REAL WORLD

Notable Quote

"It is primarily the responsibility of the Federal Reserve to maintain the stability of our overall financial system, including the interconnections between the domestic financial system and world financial markets. This obligation to protect against systemic disruptions cannot be met solely via open market operations and use of the discount window, as powerful as these tools may be."

Source: Alan Greenspan, Chairman of the Board of Governors of the U.S. Federal Reserve, speaking at the Annual Meeting and Conference of State Bank Supervisors, San Diego, May 3, 1997.

Risk Measurement

There are two approaches to risk management. The first is from the day-to-day or tactical standpoint. The second is a high-level or strategic view. It is necessary to have the capability to monitor risk from both standpoints.

Risk management requires both quantitative and qualitative analysis. Unfortunately, risk management cannot be reduced to a simple checklist, process, or number. Trying to do so can create a mechanistic approach to risk management.

The assessment of risk is a two-part process. The first part of the process is estimating the likely gain, or—more important in risk management—the likely loss, from changes in market rates or prices. To calculate potential loss, it is necessary to estimate the sensitivity of the instrument or exposure to market changes. Measures such as duration (for interest rates) are useful to estimate sensitivity to market changes.

The second part of the process involves estimating the probability of the changes. Given a potential change in market rates, the size of the underlying position, and the probability of the change occurring, the potential loss (or gain) can be estimated. Alter any of the constituents of the assessment, and a different potential loss may result.

Quantitative techniques and rigorous processes sometimes obscure mundane sources of significant risk and the need for common sense in managing them. Risks also arise from external events that are beyond the control of individual organizations.

Sensitivity

There are several methods for assessing exposure and sensitivity. The measurement of exposure is relatively straightforward, and it involves the assessment of the net exposure taking into account various positions of the organization. For example, a company might assess its exposure to a foreign currency by tracking all the various assets, liabilities, and income and expense items that are priced in the foreign currency or that fluctuate when the exchange rate changes. Exposure sensitivity provides an estimate of the likely change in value given a change in market prices or rates.

Gap Analysis

Gap or mismatch analysis measures the sensitivity of an exposure, such as an asset or portfolio, to market price changes. Exposure is measured by considering the mismatch between assets and liabilities. When there is a mismatch between assets and liabilities, or cash inflows and cash outflows, there is exposure and an opportunity for loss or gain.

Gap analysis traditionally is undertaken by financial institutions managing the balance of assets to liabilities. A financial institution that wants to minimize the gap between its assets (loans and mortgages made to customers) and liabilities (deposits and accounts of customers) will group the financial assets and liabilities into maturity buckets or pools based on their frequency of repricing or rate resetting. Maturity pools that have significantly more assets than liabilities (or vice versa) are sources of exposure and can be managed by the institution.

Gap analysis can also be used to determine currency exposure arising from foreign currency cash flows. For example, if an organization

IN THE REAL WORLD

Trading and Loss Potential

Both leverage and direction are important factors in the potential size of a loss given an adverse market move. The use of leverage, which is often a component of trading, increases the potential for loss as well as gains. Therefore, the impact of leverage is important to consider when calculating a potential loss scenario. Without the impact of leverage, potential losses are seriously underestimated.

Direction is the nature of an exposure or trading position, either long or short. A long position will obviously benefit from a rise in prices, while a short position benefits from a price decline.

has more euro inflows than outflows in a given period, but the mismatch reverses the following period, then the euro cash flows offset one another with only a timing difference. If over the course of a longer period, such as a fiscal cycle, there are more euros coming in than going out, the difference provides exposure to a falling euro.

Instrument Sensitivity

Measures of instrument sensitivity can be a useful way to measure potential for risk. Duration provides an estimate of the sensitivity of fixed income securities' prices to small changes in interest rates. Duration is sometimes used for assessing gaps between assets and liabilities, since a timing mismatch is a source of interest rate risk. Duration has some limitations, particularly that it works better for small changes in rates. Convexity, which measures the rate of change of duration, can be used to further refine the sensitivity of a fixed income security or exposure to interest rate changes.

Option delta is another measure of instrument sensitivity. The option delta measures the sensitivity of the option's value given a change in the price of the contract's underlying asset. Options that have little likelihood of exercise because their strike prices are far out-of-the-money have little sensitivity to changes in the price of the underlying asset. Therefore, these options will have a small delta. Options that have a greater likelihood of exercise will have a higher delta. The delta itself is subject to change, which is measured using gamma, or the rate of change of delta.

Scenario Analysis

Scenario analysis, sometimes known as what-if analysis, assesses potential loss by analyzing the value of an instrument or portfolio under different, arbitrarily determined scenarios.

Scenarios may be one-factor scenarios, such as a change in interest rates, or they may be multifactor, such as a range of interest rate scenarios combined with a change in foreign exchange rates. Specialized software permits several different scenarios to be run simultaneously, with the results providing information about the potential for loss (or gain) under different scenarios.

Modern scenario analysis generally assumes some asset correlation into future market movements, which is adequate when the scenarios might be anticipated in a relatively normal market. Correlations are dynamic, not static, and therefore different correlation assumptions are used in different scenarios. It is necessary to make some assumptions about correlation, but a range of assumptions should be used in the various scenarios. In a crisis scenario, markets may become highly correlated with one another, increasing potential for loss.

For example, a set of arbitrary market scenarios can be used to assess the performance of a bond portfolio. One of the scenarios is a 50-basis-point increase or decrease in yields (parallel shift). However, in reality, yield curves do not often shift in parallel. Rather, they steepen and flatten in unpredictable ways across the maturity spectrum. At a minimum, the portfolio's changes might be evaluated under different yield curve scenarios, such as:

- Parallel shift with rising interest rates

- Parallel shift with declining interest rates

- Steepening of the yield curve, assuming a normal yield curve (longer rates rise more than shorter rates)

- Flattening of the yield curve, assuming a normal yield curve (longer rates rise less than shorter rates)

- Scenarios with an inversion to part or all of the yield curve

In extreme situations or in markets where liquidity is marginal to begin with, liquidity may dry up completely for a short time. Without knowing how these correlational relationships may change under duress, scenario analysis may not provide a complete picture of the portfolio's risk.

However, scenario analysis is a useful adjunct to value-at-risk for risk measurement.

Stress Testing

Scenario analysis is useful under ordinary circumstances involving routine market changes. Stress testing is similar to scenario analysis but assesses performance under less frequent, but more significant, market changes. Stress testing permits assessment of how exposures might perform under more extreme conditions. A stress test may involve changing one or more variables or using major historical price changes to see the potential impact on financial exposures.

Large moves often take market participants by surprise, and markets may move farther and faster than would otherwise be expected. Financial crises, for example, occur relatively frequently. These large moves may be combined with a breakdown in the typical correlational relationships that are present during normal market conditions.

Stress testing an organization's exposure against extreme scenarios can be very useful. In the event that the stress test shows unacceptable results in the form of unmanageable potential losses, strategies can be formulated to deal with the unacceptable exposures. Proper preparation is key, including a risk management policy and an action plan.

Value-at-Risk

The most commonly used measure of market risk is value-at-risk. Value-at-risk is a systematic methodology to estimate the potential financial loss for a given period of time, based on statistical estimates of probability at a predetermined confidence interval. An estimate of the probability of a loss being greater than (or less than) a particular dollar amount as a result of market fluctuations, value-at-risk is commonly used to measure risk in a portfolio of assets or exposures.

Value-at-risk attempts to answers the question "How much money might I lose?" based on probabilities and within parameters set by the risk manager. One of the key advantages of value-at-risk is its ability to focus the attention of both nonfinancial and financial managers on the issue of measuring risk. It should be used in conjunction with other risk assessment tools as part of a cohesive risk management program.

Value-at-risk creates a distribution of potential outcomes at a specific confidence interval. The largest loss outcome using the confidence level as the cutoff is the amount reported as value-at-risk. Confidence intervals are commonly 95, 97.5, or 99 percent. For example, at a 95 percent confidence interval, there is the probability of a loss greater than $10,000,000 (value-at-risk) on 5 out of 100 days.

Although value-at-risk is a useful and intuitively appealing measure as a result of its ability to distill a great deal of information into a single number, it has its weaknesses. Most important, it is possible to lose more than the value-at-risk amount.

There are several methodologies for calculating value-at-risk. They vary in their need for data and computing power and in their ability to model different types of instruments. Value-at-risk calculations typically are obtained using one of these methods:

- Using historical data.

- Using stochastic simulation or random or Monte Carlo scenario generation. Monte Carlo simulation is based on randomly generated market moves. Volatilities and correlations are calculated directly from underlying time-series data, assuming a normal distribution.

- Using the variance/covariance (parametric) approach. Volatilities and correlations are calculated directly from the underlying time series, assuming a normal distribution.

One of the potential disadvantages associated with risk measurement is the opportunity for management to obtain a false sense of security. Management may believe incorrectly that financial risks have been measured and therefore are being managed appropriately.

Risk measurement is only one component of risk management, and many organizations have been good at measuring risk but poor at managing it. Markets are always capable of unexpected results. As a result, best efforts at measuring risk will never fully capture potential future outcomes. The occasional inaccurate forecast of loss may be the proverbial iceberg.

Credit Risk Measurement

Credit risk is the probability of loss as a result of the failure or unwillingness of a counterparty or borrower to fulfill a financial obligation. Exposure to credit risk increases with the market value of outstanding financial instruments with other counterparties, all else being equal.

Counterparty Ratings

One of the most fundamental aspects of credit risk management today is the careful selection of an appropriate issuer or counterparty. Issuers and counterparties with financial stability, acceptable ratings, familiarity, political stability, satisfactory geographical location, and appropriate legal form of organization are preferred. Although credit and

IN THE REAL WORLD

Credit Rating Agencies

Many companies around the world provide credit assessments of borrowers, financial institutions, governments, and debt issuers. Prominent credit rating agencies include:

- A. M. Best, *www.ambest.com*

- Dominion Bond Rating Service Limited (DBRS), *www.dbrs.com*

- Fitch, Inc., *www.fitchratings.com*

- Moody's Investors Service, Inc., *www.moodys.com*

- Standard & Poor's Ratings Services (S&P), *www.standardandpoors.com*

In many cases, issuers pay to be rated by agencies. Although ratings published by rating agencies provide some guidance, they are not infallible, and there have been unexpected and spectacular failures of rated organizations.

counterparty ratings are not technically a form of risk measurement, they are widely used in exposure management.

The global financial community uses ratings provided by major rating agencies. These companies rate specific securities offerings, typically debt, and institutional investors, such as mutual and hedge fund managers, lenders, and individual investors use these ratings to assess creditworthiness of the issuer and thus its likelihood of default. Organizations may require that trading counterparties, issuers, or potential creditors have a minimum acceptable rating from at least one of the major ratings agencies. However, although credit ratings are a useful tool, they are not a substitute for issuer or counterparty risk management by organizations.

Notional Exposure

Notional, contractual, or nominal amounts outstanding sometimes are cited as amounts at risk. In traditional creditor roles, such as lending or trade credit, the full amount may be at risk if the borrower or debtor chooses not to pay obligations. The potential loss is reduced by any residual collections that can be made.

With many derivatives transactions, less than the notional amount may be at risk. Exposure depends on whether net or gross payments are made and the amount, if any, of unrealized gains or losses that have accrued in the outstanding contract between two counterparties.

The full contractual amount is potentially at risk during settlement. When counterparties settle in full by making bidirectional payments, the failure of one counterparty to pay could result in the loss of the entire amount to the other counterparty. Settlement risk gives rise to the potential for a loss of the contractual amount.

Aggregate Exposure

Given the importance of credit risk in both derivatives and non-derivatives transactions, it is important to be able to determine total exposure to a counterparty at any point in time and to monitor these amounts against established in-house counterparty limits.

Organizations should aggregate credit exposure to individual counterparties. Aggregate totals can be netted in those situations where there is a legally enforceable netting agreement in place between the counterparties and for the transactions.

Replacement Cost

Both current and potential exposures arise from derivatives transactions. Current exposure, or replacement cost, can be assessed using the mark-to-market (current) value. Replacement cost is the cost to replicate the transaction at current market prices, presuming no settlement failures if the derivatives counterparty defaulted on its obligations. Potential exposure is calculated using probability analysis.

Credit Risk Measures

There are a number of methods for measuring credit risk, including actuarial models. Credit risk measures are probability estimates and depend on the probability of the counterparty defaulting, the organization's exposure to the defaulting counterparty at the time of default, and any amounts that can be recovered after default. These individual determinants of credit risk can be summarized as:

- Probability of counterparty default, which is an assessment of the likelihood of the counterparty defaulting

- Exposure at counterparty default, which takes into account an organization's exposure to a defaulting counterparty at the time of default

- Loss given counterparty default, which considers recovery of amounts that reduces the loss otherwise resulting from a default

Default risk is the probability that a default occurs, and although it can be modeled as an independent event, losses from defaults often depend on both the probability of an individual default occurring and the correlation between defaults of different counterparties, issuers, or obligations.

Credit value-at-risk provides a distribution of potential credit losses over a specified time horizon and examines the credit value-at-risk at a particular confidence interval. The risk manager can then review those exposures that contribute significantly to an organization's credit risk and take remedial action, if necessary.

Credit derivatives markets reflect the assessment of risk by market participants. As a result, prices of transactions between relatively sophisticated participants, such as credit default swaps, may provide insight into the market's assessment of an issuer's riskiness and a useful adjunct to other credit risk measures.

Future of Credit Risk Measurement

Major steps are being taken in the development of quantitative methodologies to model and measure credit risk. In part, the revised Basel II framework for capital requirements has led to the development of highly sophisticated credit risk management capabilities on a global scale and the improvement of existing methodologies. These credit risk measurement and management capabilities will inevitably filter down from large financial institutions to smaller organizations. Basel II is discussed in more detail in Chapter 8.

Operational Risk Measurement

Operational risk, discussed in more detail in Chapter 9, results from an organization's exposure to people, processes, and systems. Operational risk management attempts to reduce the probability of loss resulting from fraud or error. As with credit risk, operational risk is a key factor for global financial institutions in their efforts to comply with the pronouncements of the Basel II Accord, which is discussed in more detail in Chapter 8.

When operational risk events occur, while the probability of an individual operational event occurring may be small, there may be potential for a significant loss. Many of the large trading losses that have been widely reported in the media have been due to operational failures.

Increasingly, operational risk databases are being used in operational risk management. Operational risk databases are used to identify and assess potential risks, track their occurrence, model probability of occurrence and potential losses, and assist in risk reduction.

Some methods that have been used to measure or indicate potential for operational risk in financial institutions and other organizations include:

- Number of deviations from policy or stated procedures

- Comments and notes from internal or external audits

- Volume of derivatives trades (gross, not netted)

- Levels of staff turnover

- Volatility of earnings

- Unusual complaints from customers or vendors

In related areas of audit and fraud prevention, probability assessments are also used. In addition, the insurance industry quantifies particular operational risks in order to price various types of insurance coverage. However, the expertise in these areas is relatively specialized and usually beyond the scope of general treasury management.

Summary

- Risks arising from financial market prices and rates include interest rate risk, foreign exchange risk, and commodity risk.

- Risks arising from operational processes are those that involve people, processes, or systems.

- Risks involving the availability of credit and credit exposure include default risk, counterparty risk, and sovereign risk.

- Maintenance of adequate liquidity is a critical requirement for most organizations.

- Value-at-risk, a systematic methodology based on statistical estimates, is the most common measure of market risk.

CHAPTER 7

Treasury Technology

After reading this chapter, you should be able to:

- Identify common treasury technologies and their uses.
- Evaluate the attributes of a treasury system.
- Review the selection and implementation of new treasury technology.

Introduction

Technology provides the essential infrastructure for treasury. Technology is the hardware, software, and networks that provide key information for undertaking treasury activities. Financial and strategic decisions require accurate, timely, secure, consistent, complete, and relevant information to support them.

Despite technology's ability to streamline and renew treasury, many organizations spend time on activities that add relatively low value due to the poor quality of the information available to them. Many treasury activities are time sensitive, including cash management, reconciliation, payments, and trading activities, as well as the reporting to support these activities. These activities tend to be reactionary and arise from either market movements, in the case of trading or cash management, or cutoff times, in the case of payments and reconciliations. Technology is a key benefit in time-sensitive activities.

Other treasury activities are less time-sensitive although important strategically. These include capital structure decisions and relationships with financial institutions, among others. Technology can also assist in the analysis that is required to assess such decisions.

Treasury technology is not a substitute for proactive risk management and due diligence. In some cases, technology introduces new sources of risk. In most cases, there are no flashing lights or bells to alert the user to a possible contravention of organizational policy. The best technology systems are useless without appropriate monitoring and supervision.

Common Treasury Technologies

Most organizations seeking treasury technology today purchase, rather than build, solutions. This choice may be influenced by the proliferation of technology solutions that permit organizations to use resources more efficiently. Unless an effective system already exists within the organization, developing custom software can be time consuming and involve significant scarce resources, particularly in financial markets, where instruments or requirements may be poorly understood by technology professionals.

Common treasury technologies include cash forecasting and risk management software, real-time data services, including news and prices, historical price and volume data, and technical analysis and charting services. Increasingly, virtual marketplaces such as those for fixed income and foreign exchange are used for pricing and trading. The operational exposure that results from technology is discussed in more detail in Chapter 9.

Treasury activities that may be facilitated by technology include:

- Cash forecasting, including seasonality analysis and forecasts by currency, organization, or financial institution, for example
- Collection of bank balance and transaction data (typically through interfaces with financial institutions)
- Automated reconciliation of cleared payment items
- Collection and disbursement of cash (e.g., initiation of electronic payments)
- Purchase and sale of securities (trade capture), including online trading of foreign exchange and money market instruments
- Derivatives, including analysis of hedge effectiveness
- Annual, quarterly, monthly, and daily reporting, including management reporting
- Portfolio analysis and mark-to-market
- Trade finance documentation
- Straight-through processing, from transaction initiation to settlement

Treasury technology provides a number of advantages in efficiency and effectiveness. The improvement in efficiency may enable treasury staff members to spend less time on mundane tasks and therefore accomplish more. Besides streamlining tasks such as collection of bank transaction and balance data and reconciliation, treasury technology may facilitate risk measurement, scenario analytics, or portfolio management. The ability to increase reporting to meet management and regulatory requirements may also be a major factor in the decision to implement new treasury technology.

Spreadsheets

The most common technology tool today in treasury is likely to be the spreadsheet. Spreadsheets are popular because they permit users to create formulas and do analysis rapidly without any programming knowledge. As a result, they are used in many organizations for cash forecasting, pricing, and financial analysis.

Spreadsheets are relatively easy to use and flexible. However, these advantages are also potential weaknesses. Significant losses, both publicized and unpublicized, have resulted from erroneous calculations contained in spreadsheets. From an operational standpoint, errors in a spreadsheet used to make financial decisions introduce risk.

Reliance on spreadsheets, combined with lack of controls, can create unexpected operational exposures. Creating an inventory of spreadsheets and their uses, complexity, and potential for error or misuse may highlight areas of risk. Where they are used for decision making without other alternative pricing systems to check formulas, the opportunity for error exists.

Spreadsheets often are used for cash forecasting. When information is organized in a particular way in a spreadsheet, it can be inconvenient to rearrange the spreadsheet to view the cash flow data differently. In addition to the additional time required, rearranging data introduces opportunities for errors.

Reporting Software

Reporting tools are used to access data from a database. They provide users with the ability to create new or custom reports by reporting on the data in an underlying treasury database of cash flow information, for example. The report software creates a structure for the report, and every time the report is run, it reads the database data and is populated with the newest information resident in the database. Reporting software is bundled with most treasury and cash forecasting software to enable users to create ad hoc reports.

For example, in many cash forecasting software products, a database collects information from automated bank balance and transaction data downloads as well as data input by forecast users. The reporting software allows users to access these data in different ways by reading (and often manipulating) the underlying data each time the report is run. When the cash forecast is updated, the database changes, and the report reflects the revised cash flow data the next time it is run.

Report-writing software often is marketed to professionals who want flexibility to create new reports relatively easily. Although they vary in ease of use, some of the products are designed specifically for nonprogrammers, saving consulting or technology fees. Other software is more appropriate for users with a technology background.

Data Services

Real-time data services provide news and market prices and often include historical price and volume data, analytical tools and pricing, and technical analysis and charting services. Real-time market data are provided by a number of vendors, including Reuters, Bloomberg, and Thomson. Where real-time data are not necessary or readily available, delayed data, intraday, or even end-of-day updates of price data may provide an alternative, such as for remote operations or end-of-day pricing. Data generally include news, prices, and volumes for exchange-traded contracts.

An operational exposure concerns the source of treasury data. If real-time data are critical to treasury operations, and there is a problem accessing the traditional source of data, or it is not up-to-date because an exchange is closed, for example, it may be necessary to ensure alternate sources of data.

Historical data often are used for internal analysis. If historical data are important, it is advisable to confirm what data are available from the services provider. Some vendors provide historical data that go back many years, while others are more limited. Historical data availability may be limited, in part, by the existence of market data for particular markets. For example, market data for the Dow Jones Industrial Average are widely available, but often less historical data are available for certain over-the-counter or dealer markets.

Professionals vary in their requirements for real-time data. In general, large treasury operations will pay to receive real-time data because of their operational requirements. However, if some treasury activities are outsourced, there may be less need for intraday data. Real-time information is the minimum standard of information used by large treasuries, trading rooms, and professional fund managers. Data services may be provided through specialized networks or the Internet. Importantly, they may also provide the ability to enter into transactions (trades) or leave orders. Although this is a convenience for treasury, it can also introduce potential for operational risk.

IN THE REAL WORLD

Notable Quote

The founder of Reuters used carrier pigeons to relay early changes in stock prices in Europe. In the 1830s, before the telegraph made it obsolete, a semaphore line stretched from Wall Street in New York to Philadelphia for transmission of stock prices:

"Men were stationed on tall buildings and hills every six or eight miles, armed with flags and telescopes. The man on top of the Merchants' Exchange on Wall Street, where the Stock Exchange was then located, would signal opening prices to a man in Jersey City across the Hudson, and the information could get to Philadelphia in about thirty minutes."

Source: John Steele Gordon, *The Great Game: The Emergence of Wall Street as a World Power, 1653–2000* (New York: Scribner, 1999), p. 79.

Pricing Models

Many software vendors supply financial instrument pricing as part of their treasury software, ranging from simple to complex. Vendors may develop their own pricing models based on industry standards or embed pricing functions licensed from other developers into their products.

When vendor-supplied pricing tools are not desirable or adequate, third-party pricing tools sometimes can be implemented within or alongside a treasury solution. Alternatively, pricing tools can be added to some reporting software as add-ins. This will enable pricing to occur within the report, rather than within the treasury system. Pricing models may also be available as add-in tools for spreadsheets.

Bank Services

Banking services reflect the needs of treasury in an increasingly complex environment. Electronic services provided by financial institutions vary greatly by the financial institution, but they generally include these services:

- Account electronic balance and transaction reporting, either through dialup access or Internet-based service

- Payment initiation, including wire transfers and automated clearinghouse (ACH) initiation

- Viewing of account balances and transfers between accounts

- Monitoring incoming payments, such as wire transfers

- Initiation of borrowing or investing transactions

- Imitation of foreign exchange transactions, including leaving orders

- Electronic data interchange (EDI), which permits both data and payment to be transmitted between EDI-enabled organizations

Bank services may be expected to interface with other treasury technology. For example, bank transaction and balance data are transmitted in relatively standard formats, such as Bank Administration Institute (BAI) format. This permits data to be read and processed as they come into treasury software or a treasury database.

Electronic Marketplaces

One of the relatively new uses of technology is the spread of electronic trading and marketplaces. Trading is facilitated in fixed income securities, such as commercial paper, foreign exchange, derivatives, and equities, among others.

Virtual marketplaces include fixed income and foreign exchange dealing web sites. These may be operated by a single financial institution or increasingly provide prices from a number of financial institutions. The trend to multiparticipant marketplaces reflects the need for increased price transparency in markets that are traditionally less transparent, such as over-the-counter or dealer marketplaces.

Electronic Bill Presentment

Electronic trading and procurement is already commonplace in many markets, and many consumers around the world pay and receive bills electronically. Electronic bill presentment is being used in many areas, and it is of interest to many organizations for their business-to-business transactions.

Invoices traditionally have been sent in paper format to business customers. Customers subsequently made payment according to one of several methods, including paper checks. The recipient of the funds, the vendor, then reconciled the payments received against invoices sent. Information from these transactions was finally reentered into the organization's treasury and accounting systems.

Electronic invoice or bill presentment permits companies to send bills and invoices electronically and securely. Receipt of the invoice is acknowledged, and then recipients can decide which invoices to pay. Payments can be authorized electronically using the most convenient method.

One of the advantages of electronic bill presentment is the ability of the recipient to process the bill when it is most convenient, which makes it ideal for smaller businesses. Recipients receive electronic no-tice of their bills and can retrieve them invoices electronically, for ex-ample, from the biller's web site. Alternatively, recipients may go to a consolidator web site that provides invoices on behalf of many billers.

Treasury Workstations and Software

Increasingly, organizations rely on specialized treasury software to man-age many of the tasks and reporting associated with treasury manage-ment. Specialized software permits users to generate cash forecasts and create a variety of reports based on their internal requirements. Some also include or integrate derivatives pricing models. However, their cost is sometimes a consideration, and they may require additional peripheral technology and training.

Treasury software often is built on a database, and software and database may reside on a local computer for one user or on a server that serves a number of users. Web-based technology, where the software re-sides on the vendor's servers, can be used by treasury staff in various lo-cations, and is growing in importance as a component of the treasury software market.

Treasury software is increasingly moving away from a licensed server-based model to a subscription-based service model. Instead of buying and installing software on a local or network server, a month-ly fee provides access to the software on the vendor's servers through the Internet. This significantly reduces the involvement of information technology professionals, since there may be little or no need for new hardware or servers. The nature of the purchasing process and ongo-ing backup and contingency planning also change. One of the results is that the upfront cost of implementing a web-based solution is dramatically lower than for a server-based solution.

The selection and implementation of specialized treasury software, whether installed locally, on a network, or accessed remotely, can be a major undertaking. Although the process presents challenges, it also provides an opportunity for reviewing and streamlining day-to-day treasury processes.

Selection and implementation of treasury technology is a multistep process: planning, the request for proposal (RFP), and implementation and follow-up. The process of upgrading technology naturally provides the opportunity to review treasury processes and methodologies.

The opportunity to implement a new technology also provides the ability to upgrade staff skills and offer appropriate training. Treasury staff can be offered, or may be expected to use, formal opportunities for skills enhancement, both from a technology perspective and also from a process perspective.

Modules   Many treasury software solutions are modular. Customers purchase a base product or service and then choose additional modules or functions depending on their requirements. By purchasing or subscribing to only the modules that are required, there may be a reduction of cost and complexity in implementation or setup.

Treasury management modules typically include cash management, cash forecasting, foreign exchange, risk management, and interfaces. Interfaces or links to financial institutions enable the user to download balance and transaction data directly into the system. Other functionality may facilitate automated transaction reconciliation.

Customization may be required to provide interfaces to an organization's other systems and financial institutions interfaces, or to facilitate specific reporting requirements. Most treasury products come with a set of basic reports. However, most organizations find they require some additional customization, either the customization of standard reports or the creation of new reports. For this reason, the ability to customize reports is important. Interfaces to trading portals, such as those for foreign exchange and money market transactions, may also be important.

Hedge Requirements   New accounting rules and reporting standards have increased system needs for many organizations. The move toward fair value accounting for financial instruments in absence of a demonstrated hedge relationship results in additional technology requirements. For such organizations, a treasury system that is being used to price and track hedges should also be able to support the applicable requirements for hedge assessments under Financial Accounting Standards Board (FASB) Standard 133 or similar rules. Accounting issues are discussed briefly in Chapter 8.

Planning, Selecting, and Implementing Treasury Software

The implementation of a new system, no matter how much it will improve processes, takes significant time and effort. Disruptions can occur, staff members may feel overwhelmed, and costs and time requirements can expand beyond those forecast. The explicit expense and the implicit resources required to implement a new system, regardless of its simplicity, typically require analysis and justification.

Technology is not always the solution. Some treasury problems arise from issues other than technology and may not require a technology solution. In such cases, an evaluation of treasury processes may be what is required to increase efficiency and effectiveness.

Costs and Risks

A cost-benefit analysis may help to support the treasury technology decision and permit financial quantification. Although upfront costs are lower for subscription-based services, all costs must nonetheless be assessed. A cost-benefit analysis should include cost considerations in these categories:

- *Technology requirements:* software, hardware, network, training

- *Consulting and specialty services:* training, support

- *Hidden costs:* opportunity costs, staff turnover, less efficiency during implementation and testing, customer complaints, appropriateness of current staff in new role

There are a variety of potential out-of-pocket costs associated with the purchase and implementation of treasury software, including:

- Software license or subscription costs

- Annual support fees

- Consulting fees, for vendor consultants or organization's own consultants

- Training

- Custom reports

- Upgrades of hardware and/or network

- Upgrades of operating systems and/or other software

- Revision of backup and contingency plans

- Specific interfaces, such as financial institutions, accounting systems, or external marketplaces

It is also necessary to consider the risks associated with technology. These include risks of technology failure due to system or programmed "bugs" or technical flaws that permit instrument mispricing, incorrect access to transaction approval or confirmation, operational risks arising from fraudulent or erroneous reports, vulnerability to hackers or external access to organizational data, or erroneous information downloads. These issues help to highlight the importance of involving expert individuals in the selection of new treasury technology.

Benefits

In addition to the analysis of costs associated with treasury system, the benefits must be considered. These benefits include increased efficiency and speed of operations, such as cash forecasting for treasury staff, increase in automation of routine tasks, such as payments reconciliation and reporting, and new tools that permit more sophisticated analysis, such as risk management.

Some of the other benefits include less opportunity for error in data rekeying, more opportunity and tools for analytics, and customized and ad hoc reporting that can provide additional information to management, the board of directors, and stakeholders.

Specific benefits and opportunities that may arise from the use of treasury software include:

- Ability to access the market early, for better pricing and liquidity

- Fewer reversals of position because of cash flow forecasting errors

- Better record keeping and audit trail

- Enforced controls for approvals and confirmations and segregation of duties

- Greater opportunities to evidence regulatory compliance (e.g., Sarbanes-Oxley compliance)

- Fewer sales of securities in an effort to reverse position

- Better forecasting ability permitting the organization to invest for longer time periods (usually resulting in a higher yield) and to borrow for shorter time periods

- Reduction of idle or underutilized cash

- Portfolio analysis tools and reporting

- Risk management tools and reporting

- Interface with trading portals and straight-through processing

Planning

At the planning stage, the decision is made whether technology is actually required, or whether a change in process or operations is needed. Next, decisions need to be made about buying or acquiring a product that already exists versus building new technologies in-house. Other considerations include treasury staff experience and opportunities for streamlining processes, as well as other vendor relationships.

A needs analysis should determine exactly what the organization's requirements are and how they can be met. This analysis involves an assessment of the current capabilities, those capabilities that are missing but considered to be critical ("must have"), and those that would be beneficial but not essential ("nice to have").

Involvement of the key players within the organization that will use or be impacted by the new technology is essential. Key players include treasury, management, information technology, accounting, audit, and legal representatives. Discussions with current financial institutions may also be helpful. Determining the specific requirements of a new system is a key component of the success of a selection and implementation process. Considerations might include:

- Minimum requirements include essential functions that are currently performed, plus functionality that is clearly lacking

- Additional value-added functions, such as nice-to-have items and functions that might be used today or in the future

- Requirements of branches and remote operations that might be streamlined by having access to functionality that currently is not available to them

- Reporting requirements

- Accounting requirements, including interfaces to the general ledger, for example

- Accuracy of the pricing models and the flexibility to the user

The first and most important step in any major project, such as selecting and implementing treasury technology, is a determination of the objectives of the project. The objectives should be carefully determined and clearly stated. For example, the objective may be to automate portions of the cash forecasting process or to provide risk management analytics where none currently exist. The development of objectives will necessarily be preceded by discussion with key individuals in the organization.

Objectives are an important starting point to guide the determination of specific requirements, cost-benefit analysis, potential trade-offs, and the eventual evaluation of the project's success. Although objectives may be augmented or modified as opportunities for streamlining business process present themselves during the project, lack of clear objectives may weaken internal support for the project and the odds of its eventual success.

Once the project's objectives have been determined, it is necessary to determine technology requirements. This requires gathering information and an assessment of information/data/system requirements, any necessary interfaces to communicate with other systems, and support for various types of financial instruments and transactions. In some cases, technology may not be the major problem. Instead, it might be necessary to refine treasury processes.

Request for Proposal

A request for proposal (RFP) is a formal document used to determine the fit between the buyer's technology requirements and a vendor's product and service offerings. Usually it consists of a summary of the organization's business activities and a series of questions designed to determine whether and how the product or service will meet its needs. Request for pricing and company financial and legal information is also included. RFPs are sent to those vendors that appear likely to meet the organization's needs and that are expected to be within an acceptable price level. It may be helpful to have legal or technology input into the wording of the RFP document.

The development of an RFP requires some planning and a clear view of the objectives of the undertaking. An understanding of available treasury functionality is important, since it will guide the types of questions asked. For this reason, an internal review of the functionality of competing systems is a good starting point for those involved with developing the RFP and selection.

In order to assess the various options fully, adequate information is required to evaluate the RFP responses. RFP templates are available for purchase or on demand, and some software vendors also provide standardized RFPs. In all cases, these should be utilized intelligently to ensure that the appropriate questions are asked and to avoid asking detailed questions about functionality that is not part of the requirements. It is also necessary to provide adequate information about the organization, its unique attributes as they relate to treasury activities, and the objectives for the project.

The treasury system RFP has several sections to it, including an executive summary, background information about the organization and business operations, functional treasury requirements and questions, and technical (information technology and network) questions. In some cases, external consultants are used to help define requirements, draft RFP questions, evaluate responses, and provide a recommendation. In other cases, internal resources are used.

Selecting and Implementing New Treasury Technology

The process of technology selection and implementation generally consists of three stages: planning, RFP and selection, and implementation and follow-up. The process includes these steps:

Step 1 Perform a needs analysis: assess the needs and objectives of the project, including buy versus build. Conduct basic market research about vendors and products.

Step 2 Determine requirements, develop communication protocol.

Step 3 Identify potential vendors. Use industry liaisons, demonstrations, and evaluations to choose a short list of treasury software vendors from potential vendors.

Step 4 Develop RFP team and selection committee. Involve finance, treasury, information technology, legal, audit, and security professionals. Determine the selection process and criteria and which firms should receive the RFP.

Step 5 Develop and send the RFP document, providing adequate time for the RFP responses. It is good practice to contact the vendors to determine their interest in responding to the RFP prior to sending it. Any discussion that could provide additional information unfairly to particular vendors must be avoided.

continued on next page

TIPS & TECHNIQUES CONTINUED

Step 6 Be available for additional information requests and practice good ethics in all stages of the selection and implementation process by sending identical information to all RFP respondents, honoring deadlines, and preventing the sharing of information between respondents.

Step 7 Check references, select the winning vendor, negotiate the legal agreements, and prepare for implementation.

In general, a mix of question types in the RFP will provide better information for evaluation than simple yes/no question types. If a question is not asked in a way that permits an appropriate assessment of the answers, time and resources will be wasted in trying to evaluate the resultant answers from competing vendors. Before the RFP is developed, a thorough discussion and input of potential treasury system users must be undertaken to ensure that all their concerns and priorities are covered.

It is important to practice good ethics in the selection and implementation process. If additional information is requested from one vendor, send the same information in identical form to all of the RFP respondents (vendors), without revealing the identity of other vendors. In addition, honor cutoff times and deadlines for all, and do not intentionally or inadvertently share price or system information between vendors.

Evaluating Responses

Once RFP respondents have had time to send in proposals, the evaluation process begins. Ideally, an evaluation committee should be involved in the recommendation of a decision to management and the board.

Vendor selection decisions should incorporate fiscal responsibility, protect stakeholders, and improve efficiency and effectiveness. When the decisions finally are made, they should be communicated clearly to everyone involved. Information should be transmitted in a timely manner and include schedules, responsibilities, and incentives for completion, if any.

Some technology considerations that might be part of the evaluation process include:

- Integration ability with other internal/external systems (e.g., trading, financial institution, accounting and general ledger, commodity pricing, accounts payable or receivable, external portals, or custodial)

- Availability and cost of training to facilitate use of the new system

- Need for, and cost of, customized reports and the format in which they will be provided

- Multiple user requirements

- Handling of system "bugs": How will they be handled by the vendor? Is there a requirement for them to be fixed within a particular time frame?

A decision should not be made without checking vendor references, financial stability, and contingency plans. For example, some contracts require computer code to be held in escrow. These items should be considered at the outset and discussed with legal counsel where necessary. Legal can also assist with the important negotiation with the chosen vendor. Negotiation will include when implementation and any customization are to occur, fees, schedules, and other issues.

Implementation

Most implementations involve unexpected challenges. One common problem is known as scope expansion or "scope creep." Anyone who has undertaken home renovations will recognize the opportunities for scope expansion. The initial scope of the project is increased by incremental amounts until it results in serious problems meeting the predetermined budget and timelines. Scope creep also occurs in treasury technology projects.

However, the planning, selection, and implementation of treasury technology offer ideal opportunities to revisit and rethink treasury processes. In some cases, processes are made ineffective by changes in technology, and new processes are necessary to protect data and assets in the new environment. In other cases, processes were weak or lacking, and a review as part of an implementation provides an opportunity to rectify the problem.

As with any technology change, challenges may involve the new technology's ability to communicate or exchange data with other existing technologies or systems. In many cases, these challenges can be managed effectively by involving internal information technology (IT) professionals at an early stage of the project. Ensuring they have adequate information and an opportunity to ask pertinent questions or address concerns will also help to ensure that important systems have the capability to communicate with new technology. It is important to involve experts to assess protection against fraud and error and in disaster recovery. As with IT professionals, they should be brought in at the planning stage, long before implementation.

The implementation stage includes:

- Implement, train, and perform user acceptance testing of the chosen solution.

- Develop and test new reports and reconcile them against existing reports over a period of time to ensure accuracy.

- Follow-up with users and affected individuals to ensure that system and reports are functioning adequately.

- Celebrate success and communicate change to everyone involved.

Replicating existing reports from the current environment to the new technology environment may involve a cost. The redesign of existing reports should include an analysis of whether the reports are still necessary. In some cases, reports predate treasury employees and provide little or no information to current employees. Other reports that are clearly critical to an effective functioning of treasury may not yet exist.

The implementation of a significant new technology system can involve very human costs. Longtime staff members may feel threatened or challenged by the new environment. Some staff members may not have the training or knowledge to utilize new capabilities, such as detailed risk analysis. Others may resent working longer hours or overtime during implementation or testing, particularly if they do not see the immediate benefits for themselves. These are real issues, and the visible support of management is critical to ensuring a good outcome. If staff members feel that management is not committed, they will be less inclined to participate fully.

Some of these problems can be managed by understanding the likelihood of their occurrence and taking steps along the way to manage them. In other cases, internal or external consultants can be used as an additional resource to ensure that issues are addressed and problems fixed. However, the use of such specialists does not release the organization's management from a need for public support of the project. As with perceptions of management, if staff members believe that the project is in jeopardy and it is subsequently outsourced to a consultant, they may look for reasons not to support it. Proper planning will increase the probability of a successful outcome.

Summary

- Common treasury technologies include cash forecasting and risk management software, real-time data services, and electronic marketplaces.

- The request for proposal (RFP) can facilitate a better selection of treasury software than a less formal approach.

- Selection and implementation of treasury technology involves planning, the request for proposal, and implementation.

CHAPTER 8

Financial and Regulatory Influences

After reading this chapter, you should be able to:

- Understand the importance of relationships with financial institutions.

- Identify strengths and weaknesses of various types of financial institutions.

- Evaluate opportunities to improve relationships with financial institutions.

Introduction

An organization's relationships with its financial institutions are often as important to its success as its relationship with customers. Many of the activities and transactions of an organization are difficult or impossible without the involvement of a financial institution.

Financial Institution Relationships

Financial institutions are regulated domestically by banking or financial authorities. They may be regulated locally, as at the state level, or at a national level. To a treasury operation, financial institutions are critical since they provide many services that would otherwise be difficult or impossible to obtain, such as bank accounts, wire transfers, and lines of credit.

The most significant interaction most organizations have with their financial institutions exists through treasury. The choice of a financial institution is a strategic one and may involve senior management and the board of directors. In addition, the proactive management of an organization's relationship with a financial institution is an activity usually handled by finance and treasury management.

Relationship or Account Manager

The role of the relationship manager or account manager is multifaceted and involves many aspects of the relationship between a financial institution and its clients. Although the individual may have extensive financial services experience, relationship or account managers often function as knowledgeable generalists, bringing together specialists as needed from diverse areas within the financial institution. They also represent their clients internally to the various parts of the financial institution.

Conflicts and Ethics

Within financial institution relationships, as in other key relationships, there exist potential conflicts of interest with treasury staff members. For example, a potential conflict might arise if preferential treatment were given to a treasury employee's personal financial accounts in exchange for the organization's treasury business.

It is important that management help staff members to identify potential conflicts of interest and provide alternative choices of action. Conflicts can impair decision making and the interests of shareholders and stakeholders. In addition, the acceptance of minor conflicts can lead to more serious conflicts of interest.

Ethical considerations are important for treasury staffers. Although treasury staff members must act in an ethical manner at all times in their relationships with other organizations, it is often the relationship with financial institutions that has the most immediacy. The examples set by senior management and the board typically will shape the behavior of others within the organization. Treasury must conduct itself with the highest level of ethics in its dealings with financial institutions and others.

Selecting Financial Institutions

Conducting a request for proposal (RFP) to consider a change in financial services is a project that can consume significant amounts of time and energy. The necessity for an RFP depends to a certain degree on the reasons for undertaking it. If a complete revamp of some or all financial services is necessary, then an RFP may make sense. However, if only one service is necessary, then negotiations with the preferred supplier may make better use of time and resources, particularly if the intent is only to negotiate price.

Many financial institutions specialize in specific services, regions, and customers. If a particular service or regional representation is very important, the choice of potential financial institutions may be reduced, particularly in certain regions of the world. In addition, the granting of credit by a financial institution is often a reason for selection by an organization. Once a financial institution has demonstrated its commitment to an organization by granting credit, the organization may want to provide the financial institution with more of its banking business.

It is possible to obtain rankings of financial institutions and the opinions of their peers in several functional areas related to treasury. Although subjective factors influence such rankings, they may be helpful. For example, the international publication *Euromoney* (*www.euromoney.com*) publishes an annual poll of best financial institutions in key areas, including foreign exchange and credit research. *Global Finance* magazine (*www.gfmag.com*) provides rankings for financial institutions in categories such as country or cash management.

Managing Relationships

The relationship with a financial institution must be mutually beneficial. Treasury obtains services and expertise from a financial institution, while the financial institution is rewarded through fees and commissions for its products and expertise as well as transactional volume. Traditionally, the role of the financial institution was to provide financing. Today, many treasuries have relationships with financial institutions that do not involve lending.

At its most fundamental level, the relationship between a financial institution to a customer is one of a supplier and a vendor. As in other important relationships, the relationship with financial institutions should be managed proactively. The type and complexity of transactions and activities undertaken with a financial institution dictate how many points of contact exist, but there are usually several and there may be many.

Therefore, an important role of treasury is to manage relationships with financial institutions. The management of such relationships is important because treasury interacts so substantially with its financial institution partners.

Strong relationships with financial institutions are particularly important to treasury because of the nature and frequency of interaction. A good contact at a financial institution can provide advice on hedging, debt issuance, cash collections, and access to the investment community, for example, improving efficiency and effectiveness.

Consortiums

Financial institution consortiums are groups of independent financial institutions that work together to provide additional services and coverage that they could not provide alone. They provide linkages between the technical abilities and regional coverage of international financial institutions. By working together, they can provide additional services and regional expertise to customers. For example, some consortiums offer cash concentration services across member financial institutions, without the need for an overlay bank.

Relationship Reviews

Relationship reviews provide an opportunity to review the commercial relationship between a financial institution and its customers. The review should be a formal process that includes all of the people who are involved in the relationship. In a large organization, specialists from both the financial institution and the customer side may be included.

The real cost of a meeting with a financial institution representative should not be taken lightly. An in-person meeting with an account officer can cost several hundred dollars, when time and travel costs are taken into account, without considering the time and resources required by treasury personnel.[1] Despite this fact, many organizations take a casual view of the importance of a meeting with a financial institution, and many financial institutions do not spend the time to meet with their clients.

The value of an in-person meeting is the opportunity to share successes as well as issues, with a view to improving the relationship and the business results of both the financial institution and the customer. Topics such as fraud prevention and new financial institution services, as well as new requirements or constraints of the customer, are ideally suited for an interactive meeting. This is also an opportunity to reaffirm the commitment of both parties to the relationship.

Financial Institutions and Risk

Financial institutions are subject to a number of risks as a result of their business activities. These include market risk, credit risk, operational risk, reputation risk, as well as other risks.

Financial institutions choose their customers carefully. They may screen management and the board of directors to ensure they know a lot about a prospective customer. Most monitor their lending and credit relationships on a portfolio basis, to ensure that the financial institution is not subject to unnecessary risks. They conduct sophisticated analysis on their customer business and exposures to prevent fraud and unnecessary losses. These are key risk control measures for financial institutions.

Customers of financial institutions should also monitor their exposure to financial institutions. This includes maintaining an awareness of the financial institution's credit rating, how the institution is regulated, and possibly an assessment of the financial institution's broad exposure to sectors or geographic regions.

Many organizations also manage financial institution risk by ensuring they have a relationship with another financial institution. In addition, contracts for each services provided by a financial institution can ensure that issues such as liability are clearly outlined between the financial institution and the organization.

Global Banking

Global banking issues differ from domestic banking in many ways. Even when a financial institution partnership is chosen for its international expertise, issues that could not have been anticipated may arise.

The choice of a financial institution partner for international business is an important one. An international financial institution can open doors for the organization doing business abroad. The choice of financial institution sends a subtle signal to business partners. It pays to ensure that partner financial institutions are top quality, as their involvement represents the organization.

It is important to remember that it is not always possible to obtain the same financial services internationally that exist in the domestic country. In addition, it may be helpful to be open-minded to a different business culture. Rather than try to replicate the same structure domestically, it may be helpful to be flexible and open to new structures or banking products and services.

IN THE REAL WORLD

Notable Quote

"As the financial markets become more integrated, there is increasing focus on systemic risk—the risk inherent in the institutions that comprise the financial system. A nondifferentiated ecosystem has a lot of risk."

Source: Richard M. Bookstaber, "A Framework for Understanding Market Crisis," *Risk Management, Principles, and Practices,* AIMR Conference Proceeding, no. 3, 1999. Copyright 1999, CFA Institute.

Financial Institution Developments

There are a number of recent developments within the financial institution community. Given the importance of financial institutions in transactions, most of these developments are aimed at reducing systemic risk. Developments include continuous linked settlement, changes in payments systems, and capital adequacy requirements.

Continuous Linked Settlement

Settlement risk is a major concern for organizations trading in financial instruments such as derivatives. Counterparties face the possibility of not being paid, or the failure of a payment, during the settlement process. Traditionally, large global trading volumes resulted in large settlements between trading counterparties, of which the largest group are financial institutions.

One of the challenges is that trading and settlement occurs between counterparties in international financial centers and time zones. Settlements are made electronically, involving national payments systems and local financial institutions for final crediting or debiting of accounts.

Potential losses arising from settlement failures are exacerbated when counterparties are located in different time zones and settle foreign currency transactions. Currency settlements often involve currencies in different global regions, such as Asia and North America, for example. This may mean that settlement occurs nonsimultaneously during the 24-hour day, since it depends on local processing in the financial center where payments are initiated, exposing the counterparties to settlement risk.

Settlement risk has been a particular problem in foreign exchange trading, where trading volumes are very large. For example, the 2004 triennial survey by central banks and the Bank for International Settlements (BIS) showed daily trading volumes of about US$1.9 trillion, a significant proportion of which is interbank trading.[2]

Given these risks, a major initiative to reduce the settlement risk associated with payments arising from foreign exchange settlements is continuous linked settlement (CLS), which is supported by several dozen of the world's largest banks.

CLS Bank International is a special-purpose bank, central to the system and based in New York. The system, which began in 2002, operates a multicurrency settlement facility into which payments between financial institutions are made. CLS Bank connects to the real-time gross settlement systems operated by the central banks in each currency's home country. Within CLS Bank is an account for each currency.

With CLS, since trading and settlement occur in different time zones, it is necessary to use a short portion of the 24-hour day when all regions can connect simultaneously. CLS uses a five-hour overlap

IN THE REAL WORLD

CLS Currencies

Continuous linked settlement (CLS) is supported by several dozen of the world's leading financial institutions and has several hundred organizations using the system as third parties. CLS permits simultaneous settlement of foreign exchange transactions between counterparties, significantly reducing risk. As of 2005, 15 currencies are eligible for CLS settlement, with more planned:

Australian dollar	Hong Kong dollar	South African rand
British pound	Japanese yen	Singapore dollar
Canadian dollar	Korean won	Swedish krona
Danish krone	New Zealand dollar	Swiss franc
Euro	Norwegian krone	U.S. dollar

Current information is available on the CLS Web site (*www.cls-services.com*).

time and links to each country's local real-time gross settlement systems to settle for a particular date as though both parties were in the same time zone. CLS Bank works simultaneously with the various national payment systems during the time window when all the participating national payment systems are operational.

During the pay-in period, CLS member banks make payments to CLS Bank in currencies they owe to other counterparties. At the start of the payment period, each member bank receives a schedule detailing net positions in each currency. Payments are made on a net basis. Simultaneous settlement, also known as a payment-versus-payment basis, is accomplished as funds are credited to CLS member banks that are expecting payment.

The system provides a simultaneous settlement to both parties, providing assurance that parties to a transaction will receive value for their payment. As with the payments made by the national payment systems, CLS payments are made with finality and are irrevocable.

By all accounts, it appears that CLS has been well received. By the end of 2004, CLS had settled more than $3.6 trillion on a single record day, with $1.9 trillion representative of an average day. This represents a significant proportion of daily foreign exchange and derivatives settlement volume, with CLS also being used for money market and securities transactions.

In addition to the reduction in nonsimultaneous settlement risk, an increase in control over liquidity occurs because financial institutions can see exactly when settlements will occur. The use of CLS may also promote more straight-through processing, reducing processing time and costs.

Users of CLS include major banks and investment custodial firms operating on behalf of fund managers. Nonfinancial institutions typically participate through a financial institution. In 2005, a few banks were responsible for most of the third-party settlement volume, with many banks outsourcing to a processing bank.

Payment Systems

Payments systems link financial institutions globally, and financial institutions and their customers are the beneficiaries of high-value payment systems. The major wholesale payments systems are of systemic importance and offer finality of payment.

In the United States, two systems facilitate high-value payments. The Fedwire system, operated by the U.S. Federal Reserve, processes electronic large-value items with same-day value and finality of settlement.

The Clearing House Interbank Payments System (CHIPS) is operated by The Clearing House in New York, which is owned by a group of international banks. It processes more than US$1.3 trillion in about 260,000 transactions on an average day, the majority resulting from settlement of foreign exchange and Eurodollar trades. The CHIPS system is unique in high-value systems because it can transmit large amounts of remittance information along with payments.

In Canada, high-value payments use the Large Value Transfer System (LVTS), operated by the Canadian Payments Association. The LVTS system provides payments that are final and irrevocable, with a risk management infrastructure that is supported by the Bank of Canada.

The Trans-European Automated Real-time Gross Settlement Express Transfer (TARGET) system for high-value euro payments is an interlinking system that connects the domestic real-time gross settlement systems of 16 European countries. These payment systems include those of the 12 euro countries, plus Denmark, Sweden, and the United Kingdom. TARGET is operated by the individual country central banks and the European Central Bank. An enhanced TARGET2 is planned for 2007.

International payments systems are adapting to better manage the risks that arise from an interconnected global financial community. Many electronic systems for large-value payments have migrated to a real-time (or quasi-real-time) environment. This intentional shift may reduce the systemic risk arising from credit and settlement risk in financial transactions, as the risk of a default occurring between bilateral settlements is reduced.

IN THE REAL WORLD

Federal Reserve District Banks

Established in 1913, the Federal Reserve system is the central bank of the United States. It is made up of 12 Federal Reserve regional banks across the United States in these locations:

Atlanta	Dallas	Philadelphia
Boston	Kansas City	Richmond
Chicago	Minneapolis	San Francisco
Cleveland	New York	St. Louis

Payment systems in major countries reduce risk through the finality component of the payment. One of the risks associated with older payment systems was that receipt of funds was sometimes uncertain. Payments received could subsequently be reversed at a later date, putting the recipient financial institution and its clients at risk in the event of a payment reversal and offering little in the way of protection against payment default.

Capital Adequacy and Basel II

The impact of fewer, consolidated financial institutions has changed the financial landscape in many countries significantly. One of the particular concerns with respect to consolidation is that risk among financial institutions is now more concentrated, making systemic risk a greater potential issue.

The Basel Accord is an agreement between the central banks of major countries to develop consistent minimum capital standards for

IN THE REAL WORLD

Banking and Banknotes

A colorful assortment of forerunners to modern banknotes exist-
ed. The United States had a proliferation of note-issuing entities in
the mid-1800s, with as many as 7,000 in existence by the 1850s.
This excerpt from a traveler's notebook in 1840 illustrates difficulties navigating the banknote exchange rate environment:

> Started from Virginia with Virginia money; reached the Ohio
> River, exchange $20 Virginia note for shinplasters [fractional
> currency] and a $3 note of the Bank of West Union; paid way
> the $3 note for a breakfast; reached Tennessee; received a
> $100 Tennessee note; Tennessee note for $88 Kentucky
> money; started home with the Kentucky money. In Virginia
> and Maryland compelled, in order to get along, to deposit
> five times the amount due, and several times detained to be
> shaved [loss in changing money] at an enormous per cent.
> At Maysville wanted Virginia money; couldn't get it. At Wheel-
> ing exchanged $5 note, Kentucky money, for notes of the
> Northwestern Bank of Virginia; reached Fredericktown; there
> neither Virginia nor Kentucky money current; paid a $5
> Wheeling note for breakfast and dinner; received in change
> two $1 notes of some Pennsylvania bank, $1 Baltimore and
> Ohio Railroad, and balance in Good Intent shinplasters [frac-
> tional currency]; 100 yards from the tavern door all notes re-
> fused except the Baltimore and Ohio Railroad; reached
> Harpers Ferry; notes of Northwestern Bank in worse repute
> there than in Maryland; deposited $10 in hands of agent; in
> this way reached Winchester; detained there two days in get-
> ting shaved [loss in changing money]. Kentucky money at 12
> percent, and Northwestern Bank at 10.

Source: Banking, Modern Business, Alexander Hamilton Institute, p. 33, 1961.

IN THE REAL WORLD

Notable Quote

An excessively prescriptive approach is an invitation for regulatory arbitrage and for practices that respect the letter of the standards but violate their spirit. Hence, the major efforts by regulators to develop standards in close co-operation and consultation with the regulated communities in the private sector, to stress the adequacy of risk management processes and to strengthen disclosures. These are all welcome trends that should be encouraged further.

Source: Malcolm Knight, in "Markets and Institutions: Managing the Evolving Risk," speech at the 25th SUERF Colloquium in Madrid, October 14, 2004.

financial institutions in those countries. The introduction of capital adequacy requirements beginning more than a decade ago was a major milestone in financial risk management. "Managing risk at the source," as some called it, represented an international convergence of capital measurement and standards.

Capital requirements are the mandated minimum capital that a financial institution must maintain in relationship to its banking activities. One of the core principles of capital adequacy is that more risky activities should have more capital allocated to them.

Capital adequacy requirements were intended foremost to strengthen the stability of the international financial system, particularly against credit risk (the major risk faced by every financial institution), but also against market risk and operational risk.

The impact of the Basel Accord has been felt by financial institutions worldwide. Within the banking system, compliance has meant significant explicit and opportunity costs, with additional costs for amendments to the accord. The increased cost of capital is borne by financial institutions and their customers and stakeholders, but all market participants benefit from a more secure financial system and ultimately pay for its costs.

The Bank for International Settlements (BIS) is a central bankers' bank based in Basel, Switzerland. The Basel Accord is facilitated by the BIS and the Basel Committee of Banking Supervision. The committee consists of senior representatives from banking authorities and central banks from Belgium, Canada, France, Germany, Italy, Japan, Luxembourg, the Netherlands, Spain, Sweden, Switzerland, United Kingdom, and the United States.

An amended or revised framework, known as Basel II, was approved in 2004 and provided the opportunity to revise and improve the existing system. The revised framework involves more risk-sensitive capital requirements.

The new accord permits the additional use of risk assessments by a bank's own internal systems for capital calculations. The accord will not specify risk management policies or practices. Rather, Basel II provides options for banks and banking supervisors to calculate capital requirements for credit risk and operational risk.

Basel II is designed to further increase international banking stability by improving capital adequacy requirements. The new document will require substantially increased sensitivity of the capital requirements to risk. Basel II aligns capital requirements with risk management practices and includes three key areas (pillars):

Pillar 1. Minimum capital requirements

Pillar 2. Supervisory review and processes

Pillar 3. Market discipline

Financial institutions will determine the risk sensitivity of the various transactions on their books, including an assessment of the type of counterparty or borrower. Capital requirements will be based on application of a set of predetermined formulas to the risk data provided by the financial institutions. These data include metrics such as the probability of default (PD), the amount of loss given a default (LGD), the exposure at default (EAD), and maturity assumptions of the various exposures.

Banks can use three approaches for calculating credit risk capital:

1. Standardized approach (regulator provides risk measurement data for probability of default, loss given default, and exposure at default)

2. Foundation Internal Ratings Based approach (bank provides its own estimate of probability of default, while regulator provides loss given default and exposure at default data)

3. Advanced Internal Rating Based approach (bank provides its own probability of default, loss given default, and exposure at default)

Minimum levels of capital will continue to be mandated under Basel II. This means the total amount of regulatory capital will not change, but some banks may require less capital and others more, depending on the risk profile of their portfolio. One key issue is that banks will be required to set aside regulatory capital for operational risk under Basel II.

Although minimum capital requirements for financial institutions will not change under Basel II, risk measurement will change. Important changes in the treatment of credit risk will include the recognition that collateral, guarantees, and credit derivatives can be used for credit risk mitigation. In addition, given the importance of retail lending activities for many financial institutions, the accord makes some

IN THE REAL WORLD

Risk Weightings

Basel II necessitates that capital be based on the underlying risk associated with an activity. Consider this example of risk weightings for claims on sovereigns and central banks under the standardized approach. These risk weightings use ratings published by Standard & Poor's for illustrative purposes:

Credit Assessment	AAA to AA–	A+ to A–	BBB+ to BBB–	BB+ to B–	Below B–	Unrated
Risk Weight	0%	20%	50%	100%	150%	100%

changes to the risk weightings associated with retail lending, including the risk weighting on mortgages.

The accord is expected to take effect at the end of 2007 and is expected to be used by financial institutions beyond those in the major global economies. Implementation will vary by country. For example, in Europe, all credit institutions and investment firms will be required to participate through Capital Adequacy Directive 3 (CAD3). In the United States, large commercial banks will participate, while participation will be on a voluntary basis for smaller banks and thrifts.

More information on the New Basel Capital Accord, including the original Basel Accord and current documentation, can be obtained from the Bank for International Settlements (*www.bis.org*).

Accounting and Regulatory Initiatives

International accounting and reporting standards for derivatives continue to evolve toward marking-to-market and fair value. Regulatory initiatives are attempting to reduce fraudulent activities and reporting, particularly those introduced with the Sarbanes-Oxley Act in the United States and the additional requirements of other countries following Sarbanes-Oxley.

Many organizations have incurred costs in the shift in the accounting treatment of derivatives. However, the changes have also meant a significant increase in transparency for investors and lenders.

FASB 133/138

In the United States, the Financial Accounting Standards Board (FASB) introduced Statement No. 133, Accounting for Derivative Instruments and Hedging Activities (FASB 133) in 1998, and Statement No. 138 Accounting for Certain Derivative Instruments and Certain Hedging Activities.

Currently, under U.S. generally accepted accounting principles (GAAP), recognition of gains and losses can be delayed if specific hedge requirements are met. There are very specific requirements to obtain the benefits of hedge accounting. An organization may find that a hedge provides an adequate offset against market-related price or rate fluctuations, but that it cannot be classified as a hedge from an accounting perspective. As a result, it is very important to understand hedging activities from both a risk reduction and an accounting standpoint.

IAS

The International Accounting Standards Committee Foundation is an oversight body for the International Accounting Standards Board (IASB). In particular, IAS Standard 39, which deals with financial instruments, is also a fair value model. There are several areas where IAS standards differ from the equivalent U.S. standards.

Sarbanes-Oxley Act 2002

The Public Company Accounting and Investor Protection Act of 2002, also known as Sarbanes-Oxley, has resulted in perhaps the most sweeping reforms in the U.S. securities arena in decades, leading to significant changes in the way that U.S. publicly traded companies undertake business.

The changes and obligations required by Sarbanes-Oxley have resulted in significant implicit and explicit costs for corporations to comply, particularly because the changes went into effect relatively quickly. Since 2002, a number of similar initiatives, although often smaller in scale and less widespread, have been proposed or implemented in other (non-U.S.) jurisdictions.

The Sarbanes-Oxley regulations cover a number of key areas, including the creation of the Public Company Accounting Oversight Board (PCAOB), auditor independence, corporate responsibility, enhanced financial disclosures, analyst conflicts of interest, corporate and criminal fraud accountability, white collar crime penalty, corporate tax returns, and corporate fraud and accountability.

The area that deals with enhanced financial disclosures (Title IV of the original document) may be of interest to corporations:

401	Disclosures in periodic reports
402	Enhanced conflict of interest provisions
403	Disclosures of transactions involving management and principal stockholders

404	Management assessment of internal controls
405	Exemption
406	Code of ethics for senior financial officers
407	Disclosure of audit committee financial expert
408	Enhanced review of periodic disclosures by issuers
409	Real-time issuer disclosures

In addition to the Sarbanes-Oxley Act, other countries have adopted, or are in the process of adopting, rules and regulations similar to specific aspects of the act within their own markets and regulatory environments. It is too soon to determine how extensive these actions will be.

Summary

- The selection and management of relationships with financial institutions is an important role of treasury.

- Developments within the financial institution community are intended to reduce risk, particularly systemic risk.

- International accounting and reporting standards for derivatives continue to evolve toward marking-to-market and fair value.

Notes

1. Research has been reported by Barlow Research Associates Inc., *www.barlowresearch.com,* among others.

2. Bank for International Settlements, Monetary and Economic Department. Triennial Central Bank Survey of Foreign Exchange and Derivatives Market Activity in April 2004. September 2004. Available on the BIS web site at *www.bis.org*.

CHAPTER 9

Operational Considerations

After reading this chapter, you should be able to:

- Define operational risk and how it arises.
- Identify strategies and practices that are sources of operational risk.
- Suggest some methods to manage various operational considerations.

Introduction

The major risks faced by most organizations are financial market risk, credit risk, and operational risk. Operational risk arises from the activities of an organization in three key areas: (1) people, (2) processes, and (3) technology.

Although operational risk often has been loosely defined and quantified, recent events and regulatory changes have shifted the focus to operational risk. Operational risk is a key determinant for global financial institutions in their efforts to comply with the pronouncements of the Basel II Accord. For other organizations, operational risk has undergone a radical makeover as a result of the requirements inherent in legislation such as Sarbanes-Oxley.

The critical issues that impact how organizations respond to operational risk are very complex and diverse. This discussion is not meant to cover every operational failure but rather to facilitate discussion about the types and breadth of operational issues.

How Does Operational Risk Arise?

In a February 2003 report on operational risk, the Bank for International Settlements (BIS) identified a number of event types that could result in substantial losses for banks. These included internal fraud, external fraud, employment practices and workplace safety, clients, products, and business practices, damage to physical assets, business disruption and system failures, and execution, delivery, and process management.[1] Although the report was aimed at a bank audience, the discussions provide an excellent starting point for operational risk considerations.

IN THE REAL WORLD

Operational Risk Defined

The risk of loss resulting from inadequate or failed internal processes, people, and systems or from external events.

Source: "Trends in Operational Risk Management and Regulatory Capital," from *Operational Risk Transfer Across Financial Sectors,* Joint Forum Basel Committee on Banking Supervision and International Organization of Securities Commissions (IOSCO), and International Association of Insurance Supervisors, August 2003.

Many of the major financial losses that have been reported in the media, such as large derivatives losses, have been exacerbated by or resulted from operational failings. These operational failures often permitted losses to occur or accumulate. In addition, many risks that an organization faces cross boundaries and involve more than one type of risk: both credit risk and operational risk, for example.

The ability to manage operational risk requires knowledge of processes, systems, and personnel and the opportunities for misinformation or errors to occur. It requires management to ensure that policies, processes, and procedures have been established, clearly documented, and followed.

The approach taken to managing operational risk depends to a great degree on the size, activities, and risk factors of the organization. However, some principles can be used to create a framework for managing operational risk, including:

- Board of directors' understanding of operational risk as a distinct risk category

- Identification and assessment of operational risks in all product lines, processes, systems, and activities, with an operational risk assessment before introducing new ones

- Policies, processes, and procedures to control or reduce operational risk, periodically reviewed, in conjunction with the organization's risk tolerance

- Contingency and continuity plans in the event of severe business disruption

- Consistent implementation of operational risk management framework throughout the organization

- Development of an operational risk framework that is subject to audit by competent, independent staff

Losses resulting from operational exposure do not always occur in organizations with large volumes or complex operations. Although operational risk usually is associated with large treasury or trading operations, these risks and exposures exist in other types of organizations. The complexities of financial products, volatility of financial markets, combined with the operational intricacies of an organization, can produce risks that need to be managed carefully in all organizations.

The damage to an organization's prosperity as a result of an operational failure can, in some cases, be greater than the operational losses themselves. For example, a publicly traded corporation may find that the decline in market value of its company's share price reflects badly on its ability to obtain credit, issue new securities, or complete an acquisition. Loss of confidence in management and internal controls can have far-reaching implications.

One of the challenges with risk management, and operational risk management in particular, is that many of the risk factors are domiciled with various department managers. These managers may not always think of themselves or their roles as oriented toward risk management.

People

People are critical to the functioning of an organization and, from a risk management perspective, represent some of its most significant risks. The transactions of an organization involve employee decisions and relationships. As a result, potential for error and fraud always must be considered.

IN THE REAL WORLD

Changing Nature of Operational Risk

The nature of operational risk is that it changes as business changes. The increase in automation of financial transactions decreases the dependence on people but shifts operational risk to technology and systems, as the following quote illustrates:

> As [financial institution] firms' activities have grown more complex, so too have their operational risk profiles. For example, whilst the growing reliance on automation has generally reduced the frequency of human errors at a number of firms (although a number of high profile losses make clear that people risks remain substantial), system failure risks from interconnected internal and eternal systems have grown concurrently.

Source: "Trends in Operational Risk Management and Regulatory Capital," from *Operational Risk Transfer Across Financial Sectors,* Joint Forum Basel Committee on Banking Supervision and International Organization of Securities Commissions (IOSCO), and International Association of Insurance Supervisors, published August 2003.

Due to the size and volume of treasury and finance transactions, the potential damage of a large error or fraud is serious. Personnel may be subject to pressure to outperform or earn profits, which exacerbates the risk of a problem. The risks of errors or fraud resulting from individuals or employees is also a form of operational risk.

Compensation of Personnel

The role of treasury may be as a service, profit center, or a combination of the two. An organization that does not wish to speculate on financial market movements should not motivate its employees to speculate. Therefore, an appropriate compensation structure for treasury personnel should suit the risk tolerance of the organization. This is also true for the managers who determine bonuses or other discretionary compensation. Performance for bonuses should be considered carefully. Manager bonuses should not be based on treasury profits if this is inappropriate for the risk tolerance of the organization. The same is true for assessing performance based on interest earned on money market investments. Even if performance is outstanding, funds might be better used to pay down existing debt or an operating line of credit.

Finance personnel who are compensated with a profit-derived bonus are more likely to be motivated to take risks in pursuit of enhancement of the organization's (and their own) bottom line. Treasury staff members and management should receive compensation that appropriately reflects expectations of their role in the organization. An industrial company that does not wish to speculate in financial markets will want compensation based on something other than correct market bets.

Even when employee compensation is based on something other than correct market forecasts, there may be subtle or implicit messages that accurate market forecasts are a definition of good performance. All managers should be able to identify opportunities to encourage the behavior that is warranted or desirable. Compensation is an important signal of performance expectations, particularly in treasury, where market rates and profitability can be monitored on an ongoing basis.

Staff and Management

Likelihood of fraud increases with employees who are in serious financial difficulty or who have addictions, such as gambling or drugs.

Bank Operational Risk

Operational risk is an important risk for financial institutions. The management of operational risk varies significantly from one financial institution to another due to differences in size and complexity of operations. This quote illustrates the issues:

> The Basel Committee on Banking Supervision recognizes that the exact approach for operational risk management chosen by an individual bank will depend on a range of factors, including its size and sophistication and the nature and complexity of its activities. However, despite these differences, clear strategies and oversight by the board of directors and senior management, a strong operational risk culture [taken to mean the combined set of individual and corporate values, attitudes, competencies and behavior that determine a firm's commitment to and style of operational risk management] and internal control culture (including, among other things, clear lines of responsibility and segregation of duties), effective internal reporting, and contingency planning are all crucial elements of an effective operational risk management framework for banks of any size and scope.

Source: Basel Committee on Banking Supervision, Bank for International Settlements, "Sound Practices for the Management and Supervision of Operational Risk," February 2003.

Prospective employees should be screened carefully to the extent permissible by law to avoid potential problems.

Management oversight and accountability is extremely important. Involvement of key management, as well as internal and external audit professionals, can also offer guidance in the area of staff and controls. Management must have an appropriate level of knowledge about organizational risks to develop policies and acceptable strategies and monitor compliance.

Conflicts of Interest

Management should be aware of the potential for conflicts of interest within treasury. If staff members are influenced to transact business with certain institutions, these influences may impact decisions made by staff members. Although most finance professionals are familiar with issues of conflict, senior management should communicate exactly what is expected of treasury and finance personnel, especially regarding professional relationships with others in the business.

Both actual and perceived conflicts of interest should be considered. For example, suppose treasury employees have been encouraged by a financial institution to do business with the financial institution in exchange for preferential treatment for themselves or family members. This puts the organization's best interest in conflict with that of the employee and does not put the interests of stakeholders first. To reduce potential for conflict, some organizations prohibit personal transactions with dealers and financial institutions that do business with the organization. Others provide restrictions and explicit rules.

Staff Training and Skills

Knowledgeable, well-rounded staff members are an asset to treasury. Employees should be provided with opportunities for training and skills enhancement. Achieving this may require a dedicated training budget or allocation, as well as management support for training.

Employees should be encouraged to learn about other financial activities of the organization. Cross-training is an opportunity to broaden employee skills and enhance a team, facilitate succession planning, avoid reliance on specific individuals, and ensure that other employees can step in quickly in the event of a sudden departure.

Employee rotation may also make it harder for employees to cover up inappropriate actions, thus potentially reducing the likelihood of fraud, intentional misinformation, or unauthorized transactions.

The hiring of financial personnel needs to be considered in conjunction with the required operational objectives. Highly specialized personnel provide new skills to an organization, but they need to fit the organization's culture, objectives, and particularly risk management attitudes.

Financial Institution and Vendor Relationships

Maintenance of good relationships with financial institutions and other vendors is important. Good relationships with an appropriate number of financial institutions or dealers, with at least one backup, should be maintained. Overreliance on, or a majority of transactions with, one institution or individual representative should be reviewed.

Relationship maintenance includes ensuring that correct documentation is provided for a new employee who is responsible for transactions. A written list of authorized dealing and signing personnel should be provided to counterparties on at least an annual basis and whenever a change occurs. Financial institutions should be informed in writing when key employees have left the organization. This helps to avoid opportunities for errors, embarrassment, or intentional misrepresentation.

Processes

Processes and procedures help to ensure that an organization's polices are followed. Procedures are the individual components that make up processes. Documentation of policies and procedures may reduce administrative time and provide tactical support to employees. The risk of adverse consequences can result from missing or ineffective processes, procedures, controls, or checks and balances.

Often processes are designed to catch error or fraud. However, process and procedural risk also affect hedging and trading decisions, the oversight and risk control functions, how transactions are processed, and adherence to policies.

Internal Controls

Internal controls are considered to be some of the most important tools for managing operational risk. In fact, many large losses at banks have been attributed to internal control failures. The board of directors has responsibility for ensuring that appropriate internal controls are implemented. Effectiveness of internal controls should periodically be tested, documented, and amended as necessary.

Internal controls, combined with an effective audit performed by knowledgeable audit professionals, are some of the best ways to protect an organization. Deficiencies highlighted by audit or review should be corrected immediately, and feedback should ensure that problems have been corrected.

The subject of internal controls is extremely complex and should be discussed with a knowledgeable professional. Some suggestions for implementing operational controls include:

IN THE REAL WORLD

Operational Risk in Banking

Internal controls and the internal audit process are the primary means to control operational risk, according to representatives of about 30 major international banks interviewed by the Bank for International Settlements.

Source: Risk Management Subgroup of the Basel Committee on Banking Supervision, "Operational Risk Management," September 1998.

- Involve management and the board of directors with oversight and adequate information.

- Implement appropriate policies and procedures, including limits, controls, and reporting requirements. These policies and procedures should be documented and tested to ensure they are working.

- Set up an independent risk management function to ensure that policies and limits are not violated and to provide oversight to management.

- Use internal audits to ensure activities are consistent with policies.

- Include an administrative or support function that can independently price and report on transactions, if no risk oversight function exists.

One potentially significant result of operational exposure is unauthorized or excessive trading, and the potential resultant losses. Specific insurance can be used to manage certain types of risks, and a leading Lloyds of London syndicate developed an unauthorized trading insurance policy for large financial institutions. The policy was designed to provide coverage in the event of losses from unauthorized, concealed, or false trading in excess of a predetermined limit, trading in unauthorized instruments, or trading with unauthorized counterparties.

Segregation of Duties

Segregation of duties is a standard internal control. The specifics of segregation of duties vary somewhat depending on the specific activities of the treasury team, but the general rule is to prevent any one person or someone acting in cooperation from effecting erroneous or fraudulent transactions.

Appropriate division or segregation of duties among staff members is a key internal control. For example, confirmation should be separate from trading. Risk management reporting should be separate from risk generation (e.g., trading). Separation may require an administrative or support function that can independently price and report on transactions when no formal risk oversight function exists. Other important control structures include approvals, reconciliations, and verifications.

One of an organization's greatest vulnerabilities comes from the potential for errors and fraud. If losses can be concealed, and an employee is tempted to do so because of pressure to generate profits or for other reasons, the organization is at tremendous risk, particularly since the largest losses are likely to be concealed with great effort.

The subject of internal control is complex and beyond the scope of this brief discussion. An adequate, effective audit program, monitoring, and a clear audit trail, in part derived from appropriate processes and reporting, are also critical. Liaison with professionals with audit, tax, and legal expertise is encouraged.

Communication and Reporting

Appropriate and adequate reporting to team, management, and the board is important, as is a feedback loop that enables report recipients to ask questions and offer suggestions for improvement.

Reporting and communications mechanisms should ensure that management and the board receive regular risk reports containing communication about risk exceptions, deviations from policy, reports about deficiencies, unusual losses, or anything else that would permit management and the board to better assess exposures and risk.

Reporting should be adequate to ensure adherence to risk management policies and limits and deviation from policy. Information should be available based on different criteria and detail, although this, in part, depends on the systems being used to produce the reports.

Reporting should include both exposures and risk management activities. Given the requirements for hedge reporting under various international accounting pronouncements, the need can be significant.

Forecasts and Reconciliations

Cash forecasts have a variety of purposes. In addition to their use to manage liquidity and future obligations, forecasts and reconciliation also assist in the important identification of errors and certain fraudulent items. The reconciliation of actual transactions to forecasted transactions is critical to detect errors or fraud. Reconciliation should include analysis of brokerage fees or commissions that may provide clues about trading volumes or unauthorized trading. Obviously, this function must be segregated from those responsible for initiating the transactions.

A cash forecast assists in highlighting areas of market exposure and liquidity management. Liquidity management ensures that an organization is solvent enough to meet its immediate and short-term obligations. Reminder systems or other automated tools should be used to ensure that cash flows are anticipated properly and that key payment dates are met. Other date-sensitive issues, such as option expiry dates, should also be tracked closely.

From a risk management perspective, cash forecasts should be developed and maintained for the various currencies in which an organization has cash flows. A gap or mismatch between cash inflows and cash outflows for a particular currency provides information about gaps where funding is required or to assess foreign currency exposure. A forecast will assist in determining whether a gap is a timing issue or an exposure issue.

Risk Oversight

Typically, treasury activities are overseen by one or more members of senior management and, ultimately, by the board of directors. The board should have a good understanding of the financial risks faced by the firm, provide leadership in the development of policies to measure and manage those risks, and ensure that management executes the plans quickly and effectively. The risk oversight function should be an independent function with reporting responsibility to top-level senior management and the board of directors, with a level of skills appropriate to the position. Issues of risk policy, including risk oversight, are discussed in Chapter 10.

Monitoring Exposures

Monitoring exposures through timely reporting of various risk factors and transactions provides information that can be used to assess risk. This reporting might include monitoring or regulatory changes, currency convertibility, counterparty ratings, trade creditor financial stability, margin accounts if futures or exchange-traded options are used, and liquidity. This information is useful but does not provide a guarantee of loss prevention.

Marking-to-market involves repricing financial instruments and sometimes the underlying exposures the instruments manage. It is an important risk management process. Large accumulated gains and losses should be monitored and assessed for potential follow-up action.

When marking-to-market, it is important to include all determinants of market value. For example, certain derivative products might be difficult to liquidate quickly, and a liquidity impact (premium or discount) may be appropriate. Nontraded transactions with a counterparty whose credit quality has declined substantially since the transaction was initiated might also require a pricing assessment of liquidity.

Marking-to-market should include the use of industry-standard pricing models. Pricing models help ensure that the organization is receiving competitive pricing. They should be documented and periodically evaluated against external pricing models, so that any discrepancies can be investigated. It is also useful to check that internal mark-to-market prices would be comparable to those calculated using the documented pricing models. Pricing that can be manipulated internally increases opportunity for loss.

Many standard prices, including exchange-traded financial instruments, can be obtained using a real-time data vendor such as Reuters or Bloomberg. Prices for actively traded money market and fixed income securities, and some over-the-counter derivatives, can also be found on several major data vendors. Interpolation may be required for forwards and other nonstandard exposures.

Periodic pricing or mark-to-market should be undertaken by individuals other than the traders involved in the transactions, preferably from within the risk oversight or management function. Individuals other than those executing transactions may need to become familiar with, and have access to, pricing software and real-time data. Prices should not be supplied by those responsible for undertaking the transactions (e.g., traders).

Marking-to-market is very important for the requirements of hedge accounting, since the rules associated with hedge accounting determine specifically under what scenarios hedge accounting can be used.

Systems

Risks that arise from technology and systems include those resulting from financial instrument pricing and trading systems, reliance on technology in general, payments systems, protection of data and networks, and access to files or data that can be fraudulently altered or removed.

Technology has eased many of the mundane functions associated with treasury, cash management, and trading. At the same time, it introduces new risk management challenges. To a certain extent, the nature of operational risks arising from technology depends on the processes conducted in-house. For example, a financial institution will likely have a very different set of technology processes to support its transactions and reporting than a municipal government.

The subject of risk in technology and systems security is relatively technical, and many aspects are best suited for discussion with an industry professional. Systems and networks should be evaluated in light of their vulnerability to sabotage, hacking, fraud, and error. A complex system that is understood by only one employee is a potential risk.

An organization using financial products should have the technological ability to analyze the risks inherent in those products and the underlying exposure. If staff members do not have access to appropriate technology, managing the complexities of pricing and analysis of financial risk will be difficult.

System Considerations

Operational risk arises from technology and systems. Managing this risk often involves control of access to networks and trading systems, particularly third-party systems that support both real-time data and transactions, control of access to locations where technology or networks can be accessed, and employee use of hard-to-break passwords and rules for logging into or out of the system.

Employees should be instructed regularly on how to ensure data and system security. Data should be protected through on-site and off-site data backups, including availability of a remote location in the event of a physical evacuation, and data must be protected in transit and offsite. Care should be taken if nonemployees, such as consultants, have access to key areas or systems.

The ability to conduct transactions from real-time vendor systems or through access to electronic marketplaces is a source of exposure. Often management assumes that these systems are simply price retrieval systems only, but some permit messaging and trading. Therefore, they should not be accessible by disgruntled former employees or unauthorized individuals, such as consultants or visitors. Internal and external systems should support multiple access and authority levels. Some employees may be permitted to change or modify records, others can enter new records, and some employees can only read records.

Reports should be protected against an employee modifying report parameters, such as those used for exception reports, through the use of report-writing tools. Standard reports from financial institutions or software vendors may display reports in common software applications such as a spreadsheet format. In some cases, these reports can be run and then easily edited. The integration of systems or software to manage cash flows, market risk, and credit risk is ideal.

Spreadsheets are widely used in both financial and nonfinancial organizations, but reliance on them, combined with lack of controls, can create operational exposure. Significant losses have resulted from erroneous calculations contained in spreadsheets. Creating an inventory of spreadsheets and their uses, complexity, and potential for error or misuse may help to highlight areas of risk.

Systems should provide timeliness, accuracy, security and integrity, consistency, completeness, and relevance in the provision of data to the organization and its stakeholders. As technology is a fairly complex area, the guidance of professionals in this area is highly recommended.

Special Issues in Managing Operational Risk

Merger and Acquisitions

Merger and acquisition situations can present specific operational risks. These risks need to be managed during the often-lengthy transition

TIPS & TECHNIQUES

Trading and Leverage

Special risks exist in organizations where trading, with or without the use of leverage, is involved. Trading organizations, such as dealers and commercial banks, use large numbers of traders and capital. As a result, the risks of an operational failure are naturally greater. It is critical to manage these risks proactively.

Trading can be purely speculative, or it can seek to optimize business flows. The nature of trading is similar to a continuum, with pure trading at one end and complete hedging at the other end. An organization's position on the continuum depends to a certain degree on the organizational view of risk versus return.

phase but also after the transition is completed. Additional risks arise from the fact that it is more difficult to manage risk across an organization that might be geographically distant and involve various systems. In addition, different business cultures and practices may need to be taken into account, along with potentially different legal and regulatory environments.

Centralization

Many large multinational corporations and financial institutions have centralized trading, risk management, or treasury operations. These operations manage regional, or in some cases worldwide, exposures by netting hedging and liquidity requirements among members of the group.

Centralization has certain advantages, including the potential to reduce transaction costs associated with hedging. It may allow smaller group members access to skilled professionals in the operational center. However, the biggest consideration in centralization is risk. The types of risk depend to a great degree on the extent of centralization and the specific activities undertaken. From the individual operating entities' perspective, risk arises through reduced control in key operational areas. As a result, there may be more reliance on reporting and quantitative measures. Strong operational controls and effective reporting are important in centralized organizations.

Operational Management

Operational risk encompasses people, processes, and technology, and its management requires consideration of operational issues. A few operational considerations may be useful:

- Make use of well-developed internal controls and test internal controls regularly.

- Make use of internal auditors and ensure that they are capable of auditing treasury's activities and processes.

- Maintain cash forecasts for various currencies and keep them current.

- Ensure employees have an opportunity for training and skills enhancement.

- Consider implementing job sharing or cross-training to enhance the team.

- Ensure adequate reporting to team, management, and board.

- Determine backups of both key data and employee roles.

- Maintain good relationships with financial institutions and other vendors.

- Ensure appropriate controls to guard against illegal activities, including money laundering.

- Arrange contingent processing capability if the business relies on payment or other data processing.

- Follow up on exception reporting for items that are missed, errors, or otherwise noteworthy.

Fraud

The issue of fraud, and in particular payments fraud, is a topic of timely importance. Whether through check, ACH (automated clearinghouse), or electronic wire transfer, the incidence of payment fraud is growing rapidly in many countries. The strongest controls should be used in this area, and a regular consultation with partner financial institutions should be undertaken to ensure the strongest controls available are in place.

Positive pay, payee matching, ACH blocks, and multiple authorization levels are some of the methods used to reduce, but not eliminate, risk. Where passwords or other sign-on devices are necessary, they should be safeguarded and not shared, even among trusted colleagues. A formal policy signed annually by staff members in this area may reinforce the importance of such controls.

People are the enablers behind fraud, but it usually also involves a process or system component. In addition to fraud perpetrated from within an organization, there is increasingly the risk of fraud by those external to the organization. A detailed discussion of fraud is beyond the scope of this book, but the subject should be broached with experienced professionals.

Organizations can be victims of organized financial frauds. Financial scams have variously involved fraudulent financial securities, nonexistent payments or financial institutions, and altered or fraudulent contractual agreements, among others. Individuals have been victimized by organized crime acting in the name of legitimate organizations. Treasury can be a target of such activities due to the relative ease with which large, and international, transactions are consummated. Treasury personnel should reflect on the potential for fraud in their own organization and take proactive steps to mitigate its impact. Management and the board should ensure that strong controls are in place and that treasury personnel are carefully screened.

Policies

Management and board members must understand risks in order to develop policies to defend against them. Stated policies on financial risk, exposures, and limits assist in the management of financial risk. Policies should include acceptable instruments and strategies. Limits should encompass the amount of exposure the firm has defined as acceptable risk and loss limits associated with it, and the limits on various types of transactions.

Important policy issues include:

- The existence of policies to support decisions

- Adherence to policies as expected

- Periodic review of policies for changes or amendments

Policies are developed by management, and significant policies are approved and reviewed by the board. Policies should be reviewed periodically for any necessary changes or updates. Management should be capable of ensuring adherence to risk management policy through oversight and reporting.

Contingency Planning

Contingency planning is a key requirement of all organizations. Plans must be developed, available, and updated periodically. All employees should be required to formally read and acknowledge them on a regular basis. Backup documentation should enable replacements from within, or in rare occasions outside, the organization to function in an emergency when key staff members are unavailable.

In order to create contingency plans, it is necessary to understand which functions are critical. For example, within treasury, liquidity management and risk management will be some of the most critical functions. Among other things, contingency plans typically cover staff safety, data, ability to function, and security. Treasury should have its own contingency plans that encompass both short time frames, such as might be required as a result of a flood or power failure, and longer time frames, such as that following a major disaster. Organizations should utilize the skills of an experienced professional to ensure they are prepared with contingency plans.

Professional Assistance

It is important to engage professional assistance in the area of operational considerations. These areas include internal and external audit, fraud specialists, information technology specialists, market risk specialists, and credit risk specialists, depending on the needs of the organization.

In some cases, operational risk may be partially offset by insurance designed to meet the needs of specific operational failures or breakdowns. Insurance is an important part of any risk management strategy, although its discussion is beyond the scope of this book.

Summary

- Operational risk arises through the various activities of an organization through people, systems, and technologies.

- There are many ways to mitigate operational risk, varying somewhat by the organization and the types of activities that it undertakes.

- Management involvement in operational risk management can make a significant difference in its success.

Note

1. Basel Committee on Banking Supervision, Bank for International Settlements, "Sound Practices for the Management and Supervision of Operational Risk," February 2003.

CHAPTER 10

Treasury Management

After reading this chapter, you should be able to:

- Evaluate different organizational structures for treasury, including centralization and its potential benefits and costs.

- Appreciate the importance of governance in setting treasury and risk management policies and objectives.

- Review some of the current trends emerging in treasury management.

Introduction

Treasury is unique in an organization. It is a source of many of the risks facing an organization, including financial, credit, and operational risk. However, treasury is also actively involved in the financial stewardship of an organization's assets, and this includes risk management activities.

Treasury's role in the stewardship of assets is closely associated with corporate governance. Treasury functions to execute the strategic decisions of management and the board of directors, on behalf of the stakeholders of an organization. The management of treasury involves strategic decisions that impact how an organization will achieve its objectives.

Centralizing Treasury Functions

The organizational structure of treasury depends to a great degree on the organization's approach to financial management and its objectives, as well as the nature of the organization's operations and the resultant risks. The structure of treasury should be based on the critical financial and operational issues that the board and management have determined are appropriate for the organization and its stakeholders. The organization's culture and risk tolerance support the implementation of a strategy that has been designed to deliver the identified requirements. Whether this strategy results in the decision to create a centralized global function for noncore operational activities operating like an internal bank depends very much on the organization.

Centralizing Treasury

Centralized treasury operations have been a recent trend among large multinational corporations. Many organizations that once had divisions or subsidiaries operating their own treasuries have centralized their treasury operations. These treasury operations may be partially or completely centralized or, alternatively, formal shared service centers (SSCs) operating as independent subsidiaries.

IN THE REAL WORLD

Shared Service Centers

Shared service centers are independent organizations that provide treasury services. Typically they are based in a central time zone and tax-efficient jurisdiction. The SSC provides treasury services to corporate group members and subsidiaries globally or regionally.

Shared service centers may centralize accounts payable and accounts receivable activities on behalf of the group members. The types of services most likely to be outsourced to such organizations are those that are not strategic in nature and not unique to a business location. Foreign currency netting and foreign exchange transactions, for example, often are outsourced.

SSCs offer potential cost savings as well as the ability to maintain greater control over the service offered to group members. Disadvantages tend to be related to a need for a common technology platform between the group members, plus the complexities associated with implementing such a strategy.

Depending on the structure, the central treasury may undertake passive strategies and net cash and currency requirements as appropriate. Alternatively, it may provide a more active role, offering services and products in the same way that a financial institution would. In effect, the central treasury can operate as an in-house bank to other parts of the organization.

SSCs manage exposures by netting funding, investing, and hedging requirements among members of the group worldwide. One subsidiary may have excess cash, while another may require funding, enabling some pooling of funds. Centralization can be useful when numerous operating companies have transactions in the same currency or commodity.

Centralized treasury centers usually are located in low- or favorable tax rate environments. Considerations include ease of access and costs of the local labor market, available skills and language, quality of telecommunications infrastructure, and ease of accessibility. There may also be tax issues, such as transfer pricing, as well as tax incentives available from the host country.

Regional treasury centers are a common form of specialization. For example, a global corporation might set up regional treasury centers in the Americas (New York), Europe (London), and Asia (Singapore) that provide treasury services to operating companies throughout each region. Regional coverage means that a treasury center may be operational 24 hours a day Monday to Friday.

Benefits of Centralization

An organization with significant worldwide financial exposures may find that centralizing treasury has certain benefits, including streamlining cash management, foreign exchange, commodity sales or purchases, and hedging transactions among members of the group worldwide.

In Europe, where bank consolidation and a common currency have focused interest on streamlining treasury operations, there has been much interest in centralization. Costs may be reduced through fewer transactions, fewer bank accounts, better control over cash balances, and tighter processes, with the potential for long-term beneficial impact. These cost reductions are offset by the significant additional costs of setting up and running SSCs.

Payment Factories

Payment factories are divisions or subsidiaries that process payments to suppliers and vendors on behalf of the members of the corporate group. Utilizing software to connect to multiple banks, the factory can be set up in a central physical location, or it can be a virtual office receiving and sending information electronically with group members anywhere and utilizing payment methods of the low-cost ACH (automated clearing house) type. The payment factory may also process receipts on behalf of the members.

Benefits in centralizing transaction processing among members of a corporate group include increased efficiency and reduced costs. Payment factories centralize the initiation of payments for group members and electronic banking information to support them.

The payment center maintains full control over payments and the associated cash flows and operational issues. Companies can continue to use their own technologies and send payment requirements electronically. Another advantage is the streamlining of processes, fees and charges, and efficiency within one part of the group. Savings can be accrued through lower per-transaction costs and savings from bid-ask spreads on foreign exchange transactions. In addition, the payment factory may significantly improve cash flow forecast accuracy.

Disadvantages include the software costs to connect to multiple banks and any overhead associated with setting up a central office. In addition, less autonomy regarding payment and foreign exchange decisions may be a disadvantage to some participants.

One advantage to a centralized treasury is the opportunity to net currency requirements between companies with excess cash and others with a need for funding. The situation is further enhanced when there are many transactions in the same currencies.

A central treasury may also provide geographically disparate corporate group members with access to quality pricing and the services of treasury professionals with in-depth experience in a particular market. By virtue of volumes, a central treasury may be able to obtain better bulk pricing agreements with commodities suppliers, for example, enhancing price risk management.

Disadvantages to Centralization

There are disadvantages to a centralized treasury. First, the costs associated with a centralized treasury can be significant. As a result, the centralized structure is typically not feasible for smaller organizations unless cost savings are substantial.

In addition, many operating subsidiaries resent lack of control and independence over their financial transactions and relationships when transactions are centralized. Reduction in an organization's independence and hedging choices can be a disadvantage, but perception can also play a role. Local individuals may have more information about the local financial market environment, such as currency and interest rate issues, enabling them to make better decisions. A centralized operation may have less understanding or interest in issues relating to a subsidiary's market environment.

Centralizing may also prevent an organization from developing mutually beneficial relationships with local financial institutions that may be closely attuned to the issues facing a local organization. The interaction may enhance their relationships with those individuals, providing other benefits.

It is important to differentiate reactions of individuals, such as a reaction to loss of control, from specific (and potentially conflicting) organizational issues. Operating units must be able to provide and deliver on credible operational commitments. Centralization places great emphasis on operational units that are credible in their planning and execution and the organization's access to reliable information systems.

As with other treasury management techniques, it is always necessary to consider legal, regulatory, and accounting ramifications of a centralized treasury model.

Netting

Netting is a technique to net payments across an organization, providing costs savings and reducing administration. Managed internally by software or processes, netting involves reducing the number of intercompany or cross-border payments between members of the corporate group. The benefits include a reduction of payments, reducing the costs of foreign exchange transactions, wire transfers, and delays in accessing funds. Disadvantages include issues of control for group members and the methodology used to price and time hedge transactions.

Netting may be done on a bilateral or multilateral basis through a netting center. Bilateral netting involves netting between two organizations, while multilateral netting involves netting between more than two organizations. Netting may involve regulatory and legal challenges, particularly when there are cross-border transactions. In addition, netting activities may have reduced ability to use hedge accounting in some jurisdictions. Therefore, it is critical to use professional expertise in this area.

Governance

An organization's approach to treasury management should be based on the critical metrics that the board of directors, management, and shareholders determine are appropriate for the organization and financial strategies that are relevant to the organization's business, funding, or tax situation. Key to the entire process is the existence of governance of the organization. Governance helps to determine the strategic goals of an organization, which are carried out through the organization's policies, processes, and procedures.

Management and the board play a vital role in the development of an appropriate set of written financial and risk management policies to cover the organization's activities. Policies are formal documents that guide the activities of treasury. Management typically develops treasury policies, while the board of directors has responsibility for their approval. Once policies have been developed, specific strategies can be generated that are acceptable to the organization and consistent with policy. The policy is intended for use by management and staff in carrying out their responsibilities to the organization. If policies do not exist, they should be developed.

The board's responsibilities include oversight of management. With increasingly complex financial products, regulatory environment, and global landscape, the board of directors and senior management must be capable of understanding the implications of prospective transactions. One of the challenges of treasury is to ensure that the board has enough specific knowledge and understanding of the salient risks and issues to participate in decision making at a strategic level. At a minimum, management and the board must understand:

- The financial risks being taken by the organization in the course of business, including market risks, credit risks, and operational risks

- Operational controls to protect the organization against fraud and theft, including payment fraud

- Planned financial instruments and strategies for managing financial risks

- Risks of any financial instruments or strategies

- Risk measurement methodologies and their relationship to policy

- Reporting of financial results

- Implications of acceptable exposure, risk, or loss limits

- Recognition that it might not be possible to quantify potential losses with certainty

An organization's policies are heavily influenced by its objectives. Treasury assists in fulfilling those objectives. Therefore, treasury's objectives, and its governing policies, should be aligned with the organization's objectives and policies. The formalization of policies, processes, and procedures assists in building a common understanding of the strategic direction of the organization and stewardship of its assets.

Due to its financial focus, treasury is both a source of risk and a moderator of risk. For example, treasury may be involved in transacting financial derivatives on behalf of the organization. These may be entered into to mitigate interest rate risk. An operational failure, such as unauthorized trading, could cause significant losses to the organization. It is important that senior management and the board of directors clearly understand both the various risks that treasury is involved with managing and those that it specifically creates.

Policies, Processes, and Procedures

An organization's policies provide a strategic direction to its activities, while its processes and procedures enable it to get the required results. Processes are sets of steps that together provide an appropriate activity. Procedures are individual steps in a process.

For example, the activity of hedging is to manage the financial risk that arises from changes in market rates, such as interest rates, exchange rates, and commodity prices. A hedging policy provides specific direction on the methods that should be taken by an organization in its financial risk management activities. Processes will determine how transactions are confirmed and settled, with individual procedures conducted by various individuals in the process.

An organization's management covers roles, responsibilities, authority, how business decisions are made, reporting requirements, constraints on activities and exposures, and legal and audit requirements. Each of these areas must be considered in light of the organization's goals and objectives.

Financial policies provide a clear statement of objectives and strategies. In developing such policies, it is necessary to determine broad strategic goals and risk tolerance. The existence of policy provides treasury staff and management with a mandate, which enables the organization to avoid judgment by hindsight.

There are many considerations in determining an appropriate policy, including opportunity costs of doing versus not doing anything, the costs of risk reduction or mitigation (cost/payoff profile), the skill and experience of treasury staff, and consideration of the organization's objectives and risk tolerance.

Treasury Practices

Treasury encompasses a number of functional areas. Improvements in treasury therefore involve these functional areas. These areas and considerations include hedging strategy, use of derivatives, and risk management.

Hedging Strategy

Hedging is a deliberate attempt to manage risks that arise as a result of financial market fluctuations, such as exchange rate and interest rate fluctuations. Increasingly, hedging is used to manage other risks, such as credit risk, energy price risk, or weather risk.

The term hedging was traditionally a generic term for the use of transactions or contracts to offset financial market exposures. These transactions include forwards, futures, and options.

There are several general hedging alternatives, including:

- Hedge nothing: a decision is made, actively or passively, to do no hedging.

- Hedge everything that can reasonably be hedged.

- Hedge a portion of exposures, which requires determining which exposures should be hedged.

When there is a mismatch between an organization's exposure and the hedge, the hedge may not adequately offset or protect against the underlying exposure. In addition, not all financial risks can be hedged, and hedging may provide a costly or imperfect offset to actual exposure. The decision to hedge must include an assessment of the costs of hedging, including opportunity costs of forgone gains. From a management perspective, the cost of a hedge must be weighed against potential losses without a hedge.

The objective of hedging is not to outperform the market but to reduce or eliminate risks associated with market changes. Hedging provides a temporary, sometimes long-term, solution to changes in exchange rates or interest rates. It may help to provide some certainty over costs or revenues for one or more fiscal periods, providing time for an organization to find business solutions to adjust to major changes.

There are no specific rules that determine how much of an organization's exposure is hedged. Many organizations hedge one-half to two-thirds of their exposure, and some do not hedge at all. The percentage to hedge often depends on the risk culture of the organization, including its risk tolerance. The decision is also affected by rules on hedge accounting and reporting requirements, as well as industry norms.

However, due to the specific and critical requirements for hedge accounting, the term has additional meaning. Recent changes in accounting guidelines have made the practice of hedging very complex. For example, in the United States, Financial Accounting Standards Board (FASB) Statements No. 133 and 138 cover hedge accounting.

These rules stipulate specific requirements related to hedge accounting and therefore introduce a propensity for errors.

A hedge may provide an adequate expected offset to losses resulting from market fluctuations, but due to stipulated definitions may not meet the requirements to be classified as a hedge for accounting purposes. Readers should reference the various accounting rules and guidelines for the specifics in their own jurisdiction. These issues are discussed in more detail in Chapter 8.

Use of Derivatives

Derivatives are contractual agreements, the value of which is dependent on or derived from a reference asset or rate. They act as a risk transfer mechanism from organizations that want to reduce risk to those that are willing to accept it.

Derivatives can reduce and redistribute risk among participants in the capital markets. Using derivatives to manage risk may be faster and less expensive than otherwise rearranging components of the underlying business, such as sourcing new suppliers or expanding the customer base. However, due to opportunities for misuse, derivatives use should be sanctioned and understood by senior management and the board of directors.

The derivatives strategy of an organization will naturally reflect its objectives, risk tolerance, and governance policies. Specific issues, such as the organization's time horizon for derivatives (e.g., long-term hedging versus short-term hedging), as well as its ability to accurately forecast cash flows, cash requirements, and financial markets, will also affect decisions about the use of derivatives.

IN THE REAL WORLD

Notable Quote

Not everyone is a fan of the increased volumes and types of derivatives. Warren Buffett, chairman of Berkshire Hathaway and one of history's most successful investors, expressed his viewpoint:

"The derivatives genie is now well out of the bottle, and these instruments will almost certainly multiply in variety and number until some event makes their toxicity clear."

Source: Warren Buffett, 2002 letter to Berkshire Hathaway shareholders.

An organization's risk management policy should specify what derivative products are acceptable and whether an organization is permitted to use forwards, futures, swaps, or options, or a combination of strategies. The policy should also specify whether products can be bought or sold, particularly with respect to options and related derivatives.

Risk Management

The process of risk management involves steps that are unique to specific industries and organizations. However, certain steps in the process are universal: the identification and measurement of risks, the determination of risk tolerance and strategies, policy creation, and the development of infrastructure to monitor risk and report on compliance with policy and performance.

Risk Oversight

Finance and treasury activities are supervised by senior management and, ultimately, by the board of directors with responsibility to the stakeholders. Board members should have a good understanding of the financial risks faced by the organization and should provide leadership to ensure the development of policies to measure and manage risks. They also need to ensure that management executes the plans effectively.

In many companies, a separate risk oversight role is being implemented to monitor risk management activities. Board, management, and ultimately stakeholders inherit all risks that arise from individual business units, projects, and markets. Resources are needed to support the decisions that are made on their behalf by management and the board. The existence of an independent risk oversight function gives

IN THE REAL WORLD

Middle Office

A relatively new department found mostly in financial institutions and in large corporations is the independent risk management group, also known as the middle office. The group usually features quantitatively oriented risk professionals who evaluate the various risks being taken in treasury, trading, and credit-granting activities. Risks are evaluated in real time or at the end of the day on an individual position, division or desk basis, and aggregate basis. Sophisticated risk management software is used to conduct rigorous analysis.

An independent risk management function typically reports to senior management—for example, the chief executive officer. There may also be direct reporting to the board of directors. Individual business departments provide risk reports to the risk management group. The intent of the risk management role is oversight of, and independence from, the group responsible for executing strategies.

management a level of comfort. It answers the question: Who is look-ing after risk management?

Risk Management Policy

The risk management policy is a critical component of the risk man-agement function. The policy provides and formalizes a framework for making individual decisions and reflects the organization's perspective on risk. The risk management policy is predicated on setting organi-zational priorities, which are discussed in the first half of this chapter.

The risk management policy can be as broad as the risks facing an organization and may include disaster planning, investment policy, and insurance, the traditional arena of risk management. This discussion will focus on the treasury-related risk management policy, compris-ing market, credit, and operational exposures.

Developed by management and approved by the board, the poli-cy should be reviewed and updated regularly to maintain its validity as the risks and the organization evolve. All treasury staff members should be conversant with the policy.

The major reasons for undertaking the development and mainte-nance of a risk management policy are to:

- Provide a framework for financial decision making

- Mandate a policy for controlling risk, including market risk, credit risk, and operational risk

- Reflect the objectives and constraints set by management and the board on behalf of stakeholders

- Facilitate measurement and reporting of risk to management, the board of directors, and stakeholders

Developing treasury management policies requires knowledgeable input from various parts of the organization that give rise to transactions and risk. Management should be prepared to solicit internal feedback in policy development, as well as legal or other professional assistance, if necessary.

The flow of information from reporting is an integral part of the risk management process, and the policy should also address information flow. Management and the board need adequate information to

TIPS & TECHNIQUES

Potential Components of Financial Risk Management Policy

The financial risk management policy should cover the *who, what, when, where, and how* of financial risk. It should address market risk management, as well as credit risk and operational risk issues. The policy usually will outline the objectives, specific limitations with respect to individuals involved in hedging, types of permitted transactions, authority for decision making, and other considerations. Although each organization is unique, there are some commonalties, including:

Strategic Items Related to the Risk Management Policy

- Objectives of the risk management policy

- Benchmark percentage to hedge and possibly minimum/maximum ranges

continued on next page

Applicable Standards of Care

- Prudence in the management of risk, including the use of judgment and care

- Potential conflicts of interest and ethical considerations

- Authority and its delegation

Coverage of Responsibilities and Authorities

- Responsibility for treasury transactions

- Authority for trade approval

- Responsibility for confirmations

- What constitutes an appropriate division of duties

- Reporting channels and necessary documentation

Requirements for Financial Service Providers

- Internal controls to protect against errors or fraud, and appropriate checks and balances to prevent unauthorized or fraudulent transactions

- Authorization of financial institutions, dealers, or custodians, including information and authorities required

- Minimum credit quality of derivatives counterparties, debt issuers, and custodians

- Action required when credit quality of counterparties, issuers, or custodians deteriorates

Constraints on Types of Transactions

- Types of permitted transactions and strategies

- Gross maximum dollar or percentage limit for individual transactions

- Gross maximum dollar or percentage limit for transactions in aggregate

- Gross maximum dollar or percentage limit on transactions with one counterparty

- Gross maximum dollar or percentage limit for individual types of transactions

- Gross maximum time to maturity/expiry for individual transactions

- Whether both sale and purchase of derivatives are permitted

- Under what conditions existing transactions can be unwound or removed once they are in place

Reporting and Review Processes

- Methodology for calculating and reporting performance

- Frequency of repricing at current market prices (marking-to-market)

- Frequency and process for policy review and update

continued on next page

TIPS & TECHNIQUES CONTINUED

Coverage of Other Policy Considerations

- Number of price quotes to obtain before undertaking large transactions

- Restrictions on open orders (e.g., day versus overnight orders to buy or sell)

- Requirements to support hedge accounting requirements

- Requirements for both internal and external audit, including a check of effectiveness of internal controls

- Responsibility for margin accounts if exchange-traded derivatives are used

determine whether the responsibilities are being handled appropriately, within specified guidelines or parameters. The move toward specific measures for financial risk, such as value-at-risk, is discussed in more detail in Chapter 6.

Limits should be implemented for financial risks, particularly market and credit risk. Activities and objectives of the organization need to be considered in the formulation of limits. Transactional limits might include maximum size of transactions, number of permitted transactions, and counterparty limits. If the organization has an investment management operation, the investment policy will include portfolio and concentration limits.

Trends in Treasury

Some recent trends in treasury include a move to external or offshore treasury resources, improvement of the transactions and activities that can be supported by technology, and a rationalization of financial institutions and relationships. These trends are driven by technology and changes in treasury's strategic role.

In recent years there has been a major trend toward treasury outsourcing. Although organizations may outsource some or all of their treasury activities, areas commonly outsourced include payables and receivables and cash management, including investing. Trends toward streamlining and rationalizing operations include:

- Outsourcing some or all of the nonstrategic requirements of treasury, cash management, payments, investment management, or reporting

- Centralization and shared service centers—treasury performing as a strategic business center in service to other parts of the organization, sometimes with the added advantage of tax benefits

- Regional treasury groups and centers to better service the needs of an entire region, also providing the advantage of spanning global time zones

- Increased emphasis on maximizing and utilizing cash flows within the organization, streamlining payments and collections, increasing available working capital, and demand for accurate cash flow forecasts

- Organization-wide financial risk management strategy and policies

- Centralization of currency risk management across the organization, including currency netting and in-house banking activities

- Financial institutions outsourcing to companies with niche specialties, such as payment processing

- Rationalization of bank and financial institution relationships—to reduce overlap in Europe, reduce costs, minimize administration and complexity, arrange global or regional relationships for both bank services and credit

Other trends in treasury include the growing interest and use of online transactions and marketplaces, such as foreign exchange or money market. Trends in trading and transactions include:

- Online transactions and new electronic marketplaces that serve to increase price and transaction transparency for market participants—even small market participants have access to information and pricing that only large participants had in past years

- Third-party (nonbank) treasury providers (e.g., foreign exchange)

Web-based technologies have made it easier, faster, and cheaper, in many cases, to migrate transactions to new technologies. Trends involving technologies include:

- Web-based treasury products as an alternative to server-based treasury and cash management software

- Increasing demand for integration of financial systems among treasury, risk management, accounting, and reporting, for example

- Sharing of new technologies and capabilities between financial institutions, such as payments processing or standards

- New payment technologies that permit electronic payments to be generated from mobile phones or other portable devices

TIPS & TECHNIQUES

Treasury Resources

Many treasury associations are members of the International Group of Treasury Associations (IGTA). Member associations offer excellent resources for treasury education and training. One of the easiest ways to keep up with various changes is to attend one of the treasury management conferences or seminars offered by regional or country treasury management associations. Associations include:

- Association for Financial Professionals (AFP) in the United States

- Treasury Management Association of Canada (TMAC) in Canada

- Association of Corporate Treasurers (ACT) in the United Kingdom

Other treasury resources are listed in the appendix.

The Future

The future is difficult to predict, but it often resembles the past. Based on current trends, the future of treasury appears to be a more exciting version of the present. Web-enabled financial services, electronic marketplaces removing barriers of entry in transactions, expansion of the Euro zone, and new markets based on innovations in financial engineering and technology bode for a longer, though most interesting, day for treasury professionals. In fact, the future predicted by financial visionaries just a few short years ago is already here.

IN THE REAL WORLD

Notable Quote

"The world will be very electronic. Thus not only will large-scale financial transactions be able to be made virtually instantaneously to any part of the world—we are close to that situation today—but even retail transactions in financial services and in goods will take place electronically. That is, householders will be able to purchase information about taxation, investments, retirement possibilities, or education by consulting electronic catalogues and information sources in their own home. Even goods will be able to be purchased by inspecting them on a television screen, placing the order electronically and having them delivered in a relatively short period of time."

Source: Richard N. Cooper, "A Monetary Scheme for the Year 2010," presented at conference entitled "The International Monetary System: Forty Years After Bretton Woods," Harvard University, May 1984, Conference Series No. 28, sponsored and published by the Federal Reserve Bank of Boston.

Summary

- The management of treasury encompasses strategic decisions and initiatives to streamline its operations.

- Treasury policies are designed to support decisions and treasury processes and procedures. They are an important component of treasury management.

- The future of treasury appears to include the rationalization of relationships and activities, new markets, and new technologies.

Appendix

A brief selection of resources and additional information, including associations, accounting and regulatory bodies, payment and settlement systems, central banks, and exchanges, that may be useful to readers, follows. The inclusion of items in this list does not constitute a referral or recommendation of any kind. Readers should do their own due diligence on any organizations listed here.

Associations

- American Bankers Association (*www.aba.com*)
- Bank for International Settlements (*www.bis.org*)
- British Bankers Association (*www.bba.org.uk*)
- Canadian Bankers' Association (*www.cba.ca*)
- Canadian Capital Markets Association (*www.ccma-acmc.ca*)
- Futures Industry Association (*www.faifii.org*)
- Global Association of Risk Professionals (*www.garp.com*)

- International Swaps and Derivatives Association (*www.isda.org*)
- Professional Risk Managers International Association (*www.prmia.org*)

Treasury Associations

- Association of Corporate Treasurers (*www.treasurers.org*)
- Association of Financial Professionals (*www.afponline.org*)
- European Associations of Corporate Treasurers (*www.eact-group.com*)
- International Group of Treasury Associations (*www.igta.org*)
- Treasury Management Association of Canada (*www.tmac.ca*)

Accounting and Regulatory

- Accounting Standards Board Canada (*www.acsbcanada.org*)
- American Institute of Certified Public Accountants (*www.aicpa.org*)
- Financial Accounting Standards Board (*www.fasb.org*)
- International Accounting Standards Board (*www.iasb.org*)
- Office of the Superintendent of Financial Institutions (*www.osfi.gc.ca*)
- Public Company Accounting Oversight Board (*www.pcaobus.org*)
- U.S. Securities and Exchange Commission (*www.sec.gov*)

Payment and Settlement Systems

- Canadian Payments Association (*www.cdnpay.ca*)
- Clearing House Interbank Payment System (*www.chips.org*)
- Continuous Linked Settlement (*www.cls-group.com*)
- Swift (Society for Worldwide Interbank Financial Telecommunication) (*www.swift.com*)

Central Banks

- Bank of Canada (*www.bankofcanada.ca*)
- Bank of England (*www.bankofengland.co.uk*)
- European Central Bank (*www.ecb.int*)
- U.S. Federal Reserve (*www.federalreserve.gov*)

Exchanges

- Chicago Board of Trade (*www.cbot.com*)
- Chicago Mercantile Exchange (*www.cme.com*)
- Euronext.Liffe (*www.liffe.com*)
- EUREX (*www.eurexchange.com*)
- Montreal Exchange (*www.m-x.ca*)
- New York Board of Trade (*www.nybot.com*)

News and Publications

- Epayment Systems Observatory (*www.e-pso.info*)
- Euromoney Magazine (*www.euromoney.com*)
- Global Finance Magazine (*www.gfmag.com*)

- Global Treasury News (*www.gtnews.com*)

- Treasury Management (*www.treasury-management.com*)

Services

- Barlow Research (*www.barlowreasearch.com*)

- Bloomberg (*www.bloomberg.com*)

- BRC Consulting Services (*www.bankrelations.co.uk*)

- Intria Items Inc. (*www.intriaitems.com*)

- Phoenix Hecht (*www.phoenix-hecht.com*)

- Reuters (*www.reuters.com*)

- Stewart & Associates (*www.bankservicefees.com*)

- Symcor (*www.symcor.com*)

- Thomson (*www.thomson.com*)

- Treasury Alliance Group LLC (*www.treasuryalliance.com*)

- Treasury Strategies Inc. (*www.treasurystrat.com*)

Credit and Institutional Information

- A. M. Best (*www.ambest.com*)

- Bureau van Dijk (*www.bvdep.com*)

- Dominion Bond Rating Service Limited (*www.DBRS.com*)

- Fitch Ratings (*www.fitchratings.com*)

- Institutional Investor Services (*www.issproxy.com*)

- Moody's Investors Service, Inc. (*www.moodys.com*)

- Standard & Poor's Ratings Services (*www.standardandpoors.com*)

Index

V

Value-at-risk, 151–153
  credit, 157
  historical simulation, 152
  methods to calculate, 152–153
  Monte Carlo simulation, 152
  parametric approach, 153

W

What-if analysis. *See* Scenario analysis
Wire payments:
  checklist, 36
Workstations, treasury, 170–172
  modules, 171–172
  selecting and implementing,
    172–184
World Bank, 2

Y

Yield curve:
  risk, 136
  scenarios, 150
  what is, 112

Z

Zero-balance account (ZBA), 37